Who's
Sleeping
with Your
Husband? Too

Who's Sleeping with Your *Husband?* Too

A Collaborative Work Guiding Women To Live Life Their Way

Visionary Author
Dr. Jeri Godhigh

PUBLISHED BY

Josie's Girls Lead Company
1720 Mars Hill Road, Suite 120291, Acworth, GA 30101
Phone: 888-413-7337 | Email: Info@jerigodhigh.com

Printed in the United States of America.
ISBN: 979-8-9882281-0-3

www.jerigodhigh.com

Table of Contents

Introduction

by Dr. Jeri Godhigh

Your Journey to the Authentic You!

Who Is Your Husband Sleeping With?......This is my true love story – a story of Loving Me...Of Choosing Me and loving beyond my pain.

My definition of love to myself is to confront myself by taking a look in the mirror. I need to begin and stay in healing and in silence because the only person I could control was always myself. And by doing so, somewhere in the midst of it all, I would always find Jeri again.

I had to confront myself and the person I had become. The life I was living and the aura that I presented within myself. No one could ever see the true person that I was because I did a darn good job at hiding behind pain, insecurity, lack of self-love, and the courage to show up as "Me".

Once you realize that victory is closer than it has ever been, you can begin to realize that victory can be greater than you could have imagined if you can only stay the course to be free - free from bondage, free from others' opinions of you, and free of any hindrances that stand in your way.

My favorite scripture and Word of God that I stay true to and hang to for dear life is Galatians 6:9, *"Let us not become weary in doing good, for at the proper time we will reap a harvest if we do not give up."* NIV

But You Must LIVE...

How many of you are ready to go to the next dimension?

I didn't say level. I said the Next Dimension in your life! As you might guess, going to the next dimension is going to cost you something. And I get that not everyone is ready. Not everyone will want to do what it takes to get there. It's a journey!

But the truth is that life is a journey, and you have to be willing and ready to be used by God and to go through what He has set before you. Who wants to go to the next dimension? In order to go, you must be willing to embrace your pain, your triumphs and your trials.

Embrace it, for it is the very thing that will set you free, and it is the very thing that will draw people seeking help from you. Those same people are waiting for you to show up to help lead the way.

Did you read that? I said: SHOW UP as your true authentic self!

Take a few moments and ask yourself these questions, and then work through the five steps below to measure where you are and what you need to do to get to that place of living life "Your" way.

Deep...Go Deep - What are you dealing with that may be causing you to stumble? What is it that you want for your life?
1. Examine where you are.
2. Eliminate what is holding you back.
3. Create a plan of action.
4. Evaluate your progress of where you have been, and measure where you need to go.
5. Survey your progress and keep stretching beyond your comfort level to see results.

When you are in transition - going to the next dimension - you are in a place of shedding off the old and morphing into the new.

You can never embrace the new as long as you hold onto the past. Both perspectives are true, but which one do you choose to walk in?

Until you fully know who you are and have faith in God, as well as faith in yourself that you are worthy of the next dimension and that you can do it, you will continue to be stuck. You will always see the giants and not the promise. The promise will always seem out of reach and too far away.

The problems will always seem bigger than your victory. Moving to the next dimension requires us to put on new eyes and then gain new perspectives and new faith in yourself. Until you know that you know and believe in you, things and circumstances will have you bound.

Has God told you to move and that you need to pivot? "Yes, of course!" you might say. Then change course!

Your life depends on your ability to pivot, to change, to move!
Imagine being stuck - or if you are there right now, imagine being free.

Faith or Unbelief
Courage or Fear

Have you ever felt like you are marked? Do you feel like you've had a target on your back and feel like there is always something trying to pull you down? The truth is…we are all marked. We were marked at birth… heck, even before we were born we were marked. Remember that God said He knew us even before we were formed in our mother's womb. Marked!

When something is marked, it is identified. It is set aside for something in particular. It has its destination and purpose in mind. Just like us… we were marked and destined to do great things, but somehow life just seemed to take its tosses and turns. But I want to encourage you to live.

INTRODUCTION

You are marked to live…not just any ole' kind of living, but to live with love, power, peace, and purpose.

When my mother was in labor with me, the doctor gave my grandmother a choice. She said that they could only save one of us. Either my mother or myself would be able to live. The doctor then asked my grandmother to choose which of us should live.

What a choice to have to make – my mother or me. Wow!

So, my grandmother chose my mother. Well, she didn't know me yet, so she chose what she knew, her daughter.

But I am here to tell you that I am a living testimony because the Lord chose us both, and I am here today. I was marked at birth.

Fast forward to 2009. I became really sick. After many tests and many doctors, I was told that I had an incurable disease called scleroderma. The doctors said, "Ma'am, all we can do is treat your symptoms, but there is no cure." With that diagnosis in my mind, I thought I was dead for sure.

Scleroderma is an autoimmune disease. It attacks your major organs – including your skin - and begins to make your skin so tight that you feel like you can't breathe.

In the moment all I could hear them say is that what I have is incurable. Oh my gosh…Marked, I have a target on my back. So I walked out of the office feeling like my life was over and all hope was gone.

But you see, God never took his hands off of me. As Che Brown says, "It was a Setup for a Comeback."

I was in and out of the hospital with one symptom or another seemingly every other weekend. After having to have back surgery with rods placed in my back, I hit my lowest. One day, I fell out of my bed with no one to assist me. As I was trying to crawl on the floor and somehow make my way back up on to the bed, it was surely a low point. But at that point, I had determined in my spirit that I was going to LIVE.

Live until I die!

I determined to not only live, but to live intentionally - not just waiting to die but to live because I had a legacy to leave and a destiny to fulfill.

I felt like I was tapped on the shoulder and God told me to get up and Live.

At that point, I no longer felt like I was marked to die, but that I was chosen to Live and be a vessel to help someone else to Live as well.

As long as we are alive, we are marked to leave a legacy on this earth. Your life matters!

We are commissioned to Live with Power because you already have everything you need within you! To Live with Purpose because you have a destiny in front you, and someone is waiting for you to show them the way and to Live in Peace.

The infamous Les Brown once said, "Live full and die empty!"

What a tragedy it would be for you to have lived your life and not have completed the very things that God created and birthed you to do.

So, Live!!!! You have greatness inside of You!

You were Marked to Live! You were created for this!

INTRODUCTION

Words by Anthony Hopkins... I believe are pretty profound...
Read below!

"Let go of people who aren't ready to love you yet. This is the hardest thing you'll have to do in your life, and it will also be the most important thing.

Stop giving your love to those who aren't ready to love or appreciate you yet.

Stop conversations with people who don't want to change. Stop showing up for and showing care for people who are indifferent to your presence, who display temperamental emotions, who show disrespect or block you out and keep you at bay, despite your best efforts.
I know your instincts attempt everything to win the good mercy of those around you, but it's also this impulse that will steal your time, energy, and mental, physical, and spiritual health.

When you start being yourself in your life—completely, with joy, interest, and commitment—not everyone will be ready to find you in this place of pure sincerity. That doesn't mean that you have to change who you are or play yourself down to suit the judgements projected onto you by those who do not care. It just means you have to stop bothering with people who don't want to love you yet.

The truth is that you're not for everyone. And that not everyone is for you. The most valuable and most important thing you have in your life is your energy.

When you realize this, you start to understand why you become impatient with people who don't suit you, and in activities, places, situations which don't suit you.

You're starting to realize that the most important thing you can do for your life, for yourself and for everyone you know, is to protect your energy stronger than anything.

Turn your life into a safe sanctuary where only people who are truly compatible with you are allowed.

It's not your job to exist for people and give them your life, little by little, moment after moment. Decide you deserve only true and equitable friendship.

Then take a moment to notice how things are beginning to change."

Chapter 1

Unearth the Ugly
Before You Unravel

by Jamia Ponder

BEEP! BEEP! BEEP! BEEP!

Alarms.

According to Merriam-Webster, to alarm (v) means to give warning to or to strike with fear. In other words, an alarm should alert a person of something that requires attention. It could be as small as alerting you to note the specific time of day or something as big as notifying you of an incoming intruder; either way, attention to the matter should be paid. If an alarm is ignored, serious consequences could result. For example, one could oversleep and be late to an appointment, work or an important interview or be subject to grave bodily harm.

Alarms are meant as a failsafe to protect and should be given priority and handled with care.

So, my question to you is, what alarm(s) are ringing that you currently ignoring?

Because what happens so often is we ignore the subtle alarms and hints that God gives. We hit snooze over and over again. Pushing it away, setting it aside, neglecting it and hoping you'll have just a few more minutes. When suddenly, God hits us with a WAKE-UP CALL.
And WAKE UP CALLS….
Well, those ring louder than alarms.
They'll startle you more than tornado sirens.

Most often, they rattle you to the core. You think, 'Lord, I didn't see this coming!' You didn't expect it, and more times than not, it brings you to your literal knees.

I'm sure we've all had a wakeup call at least once in our lives and if we look back, we can probably see that it turned out to be the blessing we never knew we needed.

But it was also likely riddled with pain and if you're honest, completely avoidable had you heeded the small alarm.

So I'm here, my sweet, sweet friend, with another gentle nudge.

This is your girlfriend alarm – before the WAKE-UP CALL.

You're late, and it's time to get up. And I don't mean physically because I know you've been busy. You've been moving and shaking, honey. *two snaps* You've been making your lists, checking them twice, and knocking those tasks out of the way. But let me ask, what have you done for YOU lately?

If you're anything like me, I know you've probably been hearing the messages here and there, and you feel like you're in a season of being pushed. Hurried along. And I would say, drug along. But it's because it's time to GET UP. You've been asleep for way too long. Idly cycling in the rat race of life. Sleep. Wake. Work. Repeat. Stuck in a quotidian cycle of Groundhog Day. And enough is enough.

This life can be hard, and I used to pride myself on "keeping things together," or whatever that meant. The truth is - I was and am currently Captain of the Struggle Bus. I mean hot mess express. That is to say, my life is literally held together by a hair tie...and I'm talking about the one that's been used 927 times with the white showing around the band. And if you use it one more time, it's T-R-A-S-H.

Y'all, it's confession time -- I like to be in control. There, I said it. Whether in the boardroom or the bedroom - control turns me on, aight? I am a planner, so spreadsheets, checklists, and well-planned out calendars give me the warm fuzzies. I mean, I freaking loveeee it! But here's what the last ten years have taught me...I am NOT in control. Between kids, medical school, a category five hurricane, four moves and COVID - one thing became really clear: my little planner stands no chance against the Master Planner, mmkay?

So, the real question is where do you fall on YOUR to-do list? Because for me, I didn't even make the list. Not once - but TWICE. And guess what, I had the full-on breakdown! Went through therapy, got my little self together, started a podcast, found what I loved, and felt like I really had a grasp on things. Because the previous nine years, I spent toiling the soil, investing in my husband, grooming, supporting, upholding and growing him from a $8/hour emergency department tech to a full-fledged physician; all the while, I was setting aside, neglecting, and denying myself. I worked two full-time jobs across three countries, two cities, one category five hurricane and a polar vortex with our three children in tow. Then, after hitting what should have been our pinnacle, I felt this indescribable emptiness as nine years had gone by, and I seemingly had nothing to show for it. Because candidly, his degree was built on my back.

But without a break, I finally hit my breaking point, standing in the mirror facing a woman I no longer knew. Robotically moving through the everyday tasks of life with my passion and purpose toggled OFF. Y'all, I was still filled with unresolved pain and childhood trauma that I never really dealt with! I carried it into my marriage, blaming my husband for feeling unfulfilled when I was really the issue. I was looking for him for to be the father to me that he was never supposed to be!

I. Had. Unrealistic. Expectations. And they were based on failures that were not his fault.

Sigmund Freud said that "Unexpressed emotions will never die. They are buried alive and will come forth later in uglier ways."

Simply put - those things that you think you've effectively suppressed, gotten over, the things you say don't matter, don't bother you or whatever story you've sold yourself is just that – a story. The truth is that you're a walking vesicle of pain, and every time someone bruises one of your unhealed wounds, you lash out because it hurts. The infection from your past is seeping out. And every time you snap, it's because you're triggered. The things you're holding on to either consciously or subconsciously are aggravating your soul, and the long-term effects can be jarring to you, your family, your spouse, and they're downright exhausting.

Here's the nitty gritty - you must unearth the ugly BEFORE you unravel.

And I cannot emphasize the unearthing enough. You cannot deal with what you aren't willing to face. Webster defines unearthing as an exhumation – which literally means to dig up something buried for dead. The things you leave for dead inside of a living being end up rotting – they stink, infect what's well and can literally make you sick. Unravel and separate the threads of those things that seek to keep you bound. It's imperative that you become aware of the triggers you possess.

Don't let it sneak up on you. Don't miss the small whispers from God. Don't ignore the gentle nudges He politely sends, trying to get your attention. Do the work today.

Ask me how I know. I had the finger pointed at everybody, but God took me to the mirror to show me the real culprit – and that finger was pointed right back at me.

I had to get real with the woman sleeping with my husband. And that woman was ME.

And I did. I went through therapy, dealt with unresolved pain, and even encouraged my family to begin their personal journeys to emotional wellness. Then for the next two and a half years, I seemed to manage. However, without a realistic and mindful plan in place, it's easy to fall prey to old habits.

Almost two years ago, we moved to South Carolina for my husband's residency, and I found myself once again engrossed in familial service. And y'all know what I mean by that, right? Chile - I was doing whatever they needed! I was so focused on propelling forward the needs of everyone else that I was DROWNING in the shadows of my family's success. I had forgotten all about the work I put in during therapy and stopped including the "me" in family. And not only was I drowning emotionally and physically, but bitterness was taking root like a magnolia tree planted by the mighty Nile.

And here I am writing to you, having just come up for air. My family had me consumed - or rather, I let myself be consumed by them. My first thought before my feet hit the floor and the last thought before I closed my eyes was my family.

Until I was shaken loose. And it hurt. Like hell.

And when it came, that thing side swiped me like a box Chevy going 100 mph on I-95 at 3 AM. Bayyyby, I did NOT see it coming, and it took my breath away. I felt like it took everything I had. It rocked my confidence and called everything I knew into question. An infraction occurred shaking the very foundation of my marriage. And I was left there in the rubble; broken, torn, filled with questions, confused and completely undone, staring my five-year-old self in the face feeling abandoned once again. There I was struggling emotionally and battling internally standing there toe to toe with every fear I thought I once laid to rest. Why despite everything I had done, everything I had given, set aside and sacrificed, why wasn't I enough?

My marriage was in trouble, and I was completely undone. And you know why? Because I built everything I had on it. And here's the kicker....God had been giving your girl the tiny nudges!!! But I wasn't listening. I kept hitting SNOOZE.

I just kept chugging along. Because re-prioritizing me required work. And change, well that's just too inconvenient. I couldn't make time to work out or make friends because I didn't have the time. The kids had this and hubby has that and their schedules were paramount. But in the interim, I was unhappy. Steadily gaining weight – overweight….I mean overweight-ER. *insert them side eyes right here, cuz I'm still working on it*

But you get the point. If there was an excuse to be made, I was going to make it. Because to make the excuse was easier than to deal with the truth that I was too afraid to make the change.

So, in comes the WAKE UP CALL – and this was a core shaker.

God said, "No!" He reminded me that I was supposed to build everything on HIM. Not the kids. Not my husband - not my marriage. HIM.

I now know why the hymn is sung, "On Christ the solid rock I stand, all other ground is sinking sand." Because honey, I sunk! Hard and fast.

But as the old adage goes, a hard head makes a soft behind. So you can either learn from my experience or let God give you one of your own. But either way, the unearthing will happen.

I encourage you to get sure of who you are and slowly begin to reintroduce yourself to you.

Someone might say, Jamia, I have NO idea where to start. To that I say, ask yourself the question, and you will begin to answer. Explore and try new things.
Write out what you're afraid of and then out to the other side, write the truth.

Stop the crazy things you've been telling yourself. Repeating to yourself that "no one loves me because I'm not good enough" only purports the negative things, and then you find scenarios to support. Those toxic thought patterns impact what you believe and, ultimately, what you see.

Take out the 'Woe is Me' track on Side A and turn it over to Side B.

That one is hitting on, "WOAH IT'S ME!" Over there, life is golden, and you are the bomb golden Queen you've always been but stood in the way of seeing.

Start by honestly answering these questions:

1. Who Are You?
2. What Are You Most Proud Of? - caveat, it cannot involve anyone else

If you can't – that's okay! Let me tell you, about three years ago, I could not answer either. And it was painful. Everything I thought I was and everything I was proud of was tied up in someone else. I had to start with a painful admission - I had no idea who I was or what I was proud of. In fact, I didn't know what I liked and really identified as purposeless. I was in a season of stuck.

Because I love you and want you to succeed, I'm going to give you some hints to help answer the questions above: The best place to find the answer to question number 1 lies in God's word.

Go to His word and see what He says about you. Seek out those answers, write them down and repeat them DAILY. These are your affirmations.

Now, question number 2 will require a bit more of you because pride is such a personal journey. It could be that you haven't had a soda in 10 days, maybe it's the successful completion of your doctoral program, or maybe you haven't been late to any appointments in the last year. All of those are reasons to be proud. And if you really can't think of anything, use it as a goal setter. Think of an area where you're challenged and set a goal, then achieve it. And BOOM. You've got a new personal best.

Ok sis, I see you…maybe you know who you are!! You go ahead with your bad self, BUT in this season, you're feeling isolated. Well to that, I say that's good, too. And here's why: It's because you're in a season of transformation. And that can only happen in isolation. Not everyone can handle your in-between stage. It's ugly, uncomfortable, emotional, and you're totally reliant on God.

Question for you...have you ever watched a caterpillar become a butterfly? Most of us haven't. Caterpillars don't become butterflies on a stage in front of the world. Butterflies transform in a cocoon alone. And it's tight. The closer it gets to becoming its full self, the less space there is inside the cocoon. So, I'm here to tell you that if it feels like it's snug where you are, that means that you're close to becoming your full self. You are outgrowing your cocoon, and you're transforming. Hang in there and get ready to bust out. The space you're in now will no longer be able to hold you because there's no longer enough room.

Becoming your full self is a process. Along the way, you will grab and lose sight of who you are over and over again. It's not a one-stop shop. It's a continual state of being. We always think that once we reach this particular phase of life that things will magically get better, but the key is to really LIVE in the now. LIVE with all of its hardships, beauties, failures, lessons, and losses because nothing is promised.

Life, motherhood, marriage, and being a woman of purpose will call into question WHO YOU ARE. You will struggle with your identity and purpose and so many of us fall into the trap of tying our worth to our works. The problem with that is we will NEVER be able to do enough. You cannot serve your way into fulfillment. You must first begin by being fulfilled with who God made you to be.

You are so much more than what you do and can do for people. And when we lead with our offers of service, we exchange our value for their praise.

Take a quick survey of your life and the relationships around you. How do they stack up? Are you poured into as much as you pour out? Or is there a gross imbalance in the scales? Newsflash - how others treat you is often a direct reflection of what you allow. If you allow them to overlook, mistreat, mishandle, and otherwise abuse you, it's likely because you allow it. It's time to put some RESPECT BACK ON OUR NAMES! And it starts with youuuuu because that is the ONLY person you can control. Start respecting yourself enough to insert boundaries in your life that protect your peace. Respect is defined as a way of treating or thinking about something or someone with a feeling of deep admiration. So, admire yo' own self. Admire yourself enough to say no and mean it. It doesn't have to be mean, but it needs to be firm and unwavering.

We are done tying our sense of worthiness to our level of productivity. We are done waiting for others to validate us. We are done putting life on pause.
It's time to L-I-V-E.
Rediscover who you are, identify the issues that have been holding you back, recognize how they domino into other areas of your life, HEAL, decide to choose differently starting today and reignite the passions lying dormant within you.

Accept what's been done, accept responsibility for your part in where you are now, and take ownership of where you desire to go. Speak up for yourself. It's time out for leaving your thoughts up for interpretation.

Kiss me here, there, everywhere – don't do this, that, or the other – I want this, that and these. Yes, please. Say what you mean and mean what you say with your whole heart.

We are a sum total of our experiences; they have taught us, shaped us, molded us, and in a lot of ways trained us on how to handle ourselves and how others should handle us, be it good or be it bad. But it doesn't have to impact us today.

WE CAN CHOOSE TO MAKE THINGS DIFFERENT.

I want to encourage and ignite an awakening in you to realize the power in prioritizing you. There is power in knowing WHO YOU ARE! There is power in VULNERABILITY! There is power in TRANSPARENCY! There is power in your PURPOSE! But most of all, there is power in YOU! You figure it out for everybody else. It's time to do it for you. You are more than a conqueror, and there is no one like you in the entire world.

Affirm your story IN TRUTH starting today.

Years ago, I wrote I AM affirmations for myself to remind me of who I am. I lost sight of her along the way, but I think it's worth repeating and sharing in this space for you today:

I am happy. I am whole. I am courageous. I am brave. I have no lack. I am chosen. I am called to change lives. I am equipped by God to fulfill my purpose on this Earth. I am confident. I am walking in my purpose. I am a giver. I am a hard worker. I am responsible. I am worthy of love. I am exactly where I am supposed to be. I am fearfully and wonderfully made. I am NOT forgotten. I am loved. I am treasured. I am influential. I am funny. I am intelligent. I am NOT perfect but rather perfectly imperfect. I am flawed. I am forgiven. I am a forgiver. I am positioned to receive blessings. I am more than my past mistakes. I am more than the trauma I've experienced. I am NOT a failure. I am exactly the mother that my children need. I am the wife that my husband desires and needs. I am living life by faith. I am in a place of abundance. I am gifted. I am peaceful. I am calm. I am passionate. I have the favor of God. I am healthy. I am successful. I am grateful. I am blessed. I am generous. I am empathetic. I am compassionate. I am productive. I am trustworthy. I am responsible. I am unique, and I am more than enough.

I am most proud of the woman I've become and the one I am becoming!

WHO'S SLEEPING WITH YOUR HUSBAND TOO?

Now, I challenge you to write your I AM statements bathed in truth.

And do it BEFORE you wake up undone.
God gave you something special that someone else needs.

I double dare you to walk in it.

I know ISSALOT...but you're worth it!

Love you endlessly,

Jamia

Chapter 2

Who is Driving My Love Train?
A Story of Life, Love, and Finding Me

by Stephany Tullis

"For I know the plans I have for you," says the LORD. "They are plans for good and not for disaster, to give you a future and a hope." (Jeremiah 29.11 NLT)

God has blessed me, but I have had my share of ups and downs. I've had super good and extra special good times and I've also had my share of what some might call 'the bad' times. But it seems like I've always known that God was with me and guiding me. Since God was and is in charge, I accept that He has not been surprised by any of my life experiences.

And as Oprah Winfrey would say, "Some things I know for sure." And, I know for sure that He was right there rejoicing along with me in the several over-the-top times that He graced me with. I also know without a doubt that He will never, ever leave me.

I ask myself, "So, what's the problem?"

It's simple. I'm stuck. Frozen in time. And I don't know what to do. I bet you're wondering, 'what's the story behind my story?'

Did I take the wrong train?
I did not! Because love is the answer!

Am I sitting in the wrong seat? Nada!
God has a reserved seat with my name on it.

Is the Engineer on break?
Heavens no! He never sleeps nor slumbers.

Has the Grace Train Line gone out of business?
Impossible! I know the owner.

So, what's the story?

*****

WHO IS DRIVING MY LOVE TRAIN?
A STORY OF LIFE, LOVE, AND FINDING ME

"Direct your children onto the right path, and when they are older, they will not leave it." (Proverbs 22:6 NLT)

I adopted my morning ritual from my mother, who was a devout Baptist, raised by my grandmother, a Baptist from the tip of her toes to the crown of her Sunday morning hat. Grandma was also the "Mother" of our church. We attended one of the oldest and largest Baptist churches in upstate New York. I remember sitting next to my grandmother every Sunday in her designated front-row seat.

My mother was also a claimant for a front-row seat. She was a first soprano in the church choir. Mama, as we called her (there were six of us; my youngest brother passed away as an infant), walked by faith and didn't have a mean bone in her body. She was also an avid reader. I inherited this trait from her and still love to read. Norman Vincent Peale, one of the most influential pastors of his time, and author of The Power of Positive Thinking; and, Phyllis Wheatley, the first American slave to publish her written work: Poems on Various Subjects, Religious and Moral, were two of Mama's favorite authors. Their books proudly claimed the space next to Ma's Bible on her nightstand.
I share all of this because my mother had a daily mantra. The two of us faithfully repeated it together every morning before officially starting our day—

'Thank you, Lord, for another day.

I can do all things through Christ who strengthens me.

God is in his heaven, and all is right with the world.

Today is a beautiful day. I am beautiful today.

May I only have good thoughts for the people I meet today;

and may they only have good thoughts for me'.

I'll share the significance of this adolescent memory. Would you believe that I still faithfully recite my morning greeting as I welcome the sun through my bedroom blinds? It has brightened and enlightened me every day of my life; adding pep to my step, and a smile to my face. My daily mantra reiterates my belief that God will not only order my steps *but my added belief that I will know,* with confidence, the order those steps should take. My youngest daughter adopted this tradition, and each time we joyfully recite it together, I can just see Mama smiling down at us.

And now, I still believe 'I can do all things through Christ' and even conquer the world, if necessary, when and if God presents such challenges to me. He's never lost a battle, correct?

For the last year or so, however, I have prayerfully concluded my daily mantra with a special plea, "Lord, I know I can do all things through You, but I don't know what I am supposed to do. Can you tell me, please?"

*****

"But don't just listen to God's word. You must do what it says. Otherwise, you are only fooling yourselves." (James 1: 22 NLT)

So, for the past year, I've been stuck—what the heck am I supposed to be doing? As a devout 'doer' of the Word, I can't believe that I don't know what to do. Literally.

I know God and believe that He still has a plan for me. Since he always has, why would He not have one for me now? Why do I feel immobilized by life? "Woe is me," I think. I'm restless. Frustrated. Perplexed. And I do not like sitting around "doing nothing" as I wait to hear from God. I know He will answer because He is an on-time God. But this waiting process is not my typical style.

Part of my problem is that I've never questioned that I didn't know what God wanted me to do. Why would I? I've lived and continue to live a purpose-filled life—haven't I? I ask myself. I assume I do. I've never felt that God has not ordered my steps.

WHO IS DRIVING MY LOVE TRAIN?
A STORY OF LIFE, LOVE, AND FINDING ME

Hmmm, except for some of those steps that will remain unmentioned. It would be hard for me to believe that the Man above directed me down some of those side streets, shortcuts, and dimly lit winding pathways. Whenever I periodically reflect on my life, I thank my Heavenly Father that my Angels surrounded me during those expeditions off the well-beaten roads. I am truly thankful that I didn't get lost during those 'back of beyond' diversions.

God has blessed me with an incredible career, life, family, and personal experiences.
I'm the planner.
I'm the organizer.
Everyone seeks my advice.
Everyone knows they can depend on me.
I'm a giver.
If you need a favor, ask Steph. She'll gladly do it. And I will gladly do so because I've been taught, "To whom much is given, much will be required." (Luke 12: 48 NLT).
Besides, I have to be a "doer"… I know no other way of life. But God must know that, right?

So why do I suddenly experience this recent phenomenon? I still possess and continue to use my gifts, but Stephany doesn't have a clue as to what she should be doing. Am I suffering from an unknown post-COVID life condition?

I love God. I faithfully go to church. I attend Bible Study. Morning prayers. Daily confessions. Evening prayers. What am I missing?

*****

"We can make our plans, but the Lord determines our steps." (Proverbs 16.9 NLT)

I'm learning the importance of depending on God and not on myself.

I've always believed that I depended on Him, but now I know it! It's almost like I am afraid to move without checking in for permission. I'm not quite all the way there, but I'm so much closer. I'm now waiting for this marvelous revelation of the straight path(s) I'm supposed to follow. At this point, I will even settle for a crooked one. Forgive the humor, but it reflects my current mindset and my conversation with my Holy Father. Thankfully, I know He has patience with me, and better yet, He understands me better than anyone else. Including me!

*****

"My sheep listen to my voice; I know them, and they follow me." (John 10:27 NLT)

I can do all things through Christ… but am I yielding to Him? Am I waiting for Him? Have I surrendered to Him? Or do I unwittingly relapse? Whose voice am I hearing? His? Or mine?

Am I still relying on my past understandings, or have I acknowledged and accepted that I need and want Him to guide me to my future path?

Furthermore, now that I clearly know, understand, and accept my Leader and believe that He—Has—Spoken, have I misunderstood His voice? Have I misinterpreted His voice? Did I forget what He said? Or, even worse, have I ignored what He said?

If someone intentionally ignored my request, I'd be offended. It's one thing to not hear me; understand me or not want to be bothered by me. It's another for that person to hear me and disregard the seriousness of the request or suggestion without acknowledging that they heard me.

And it's even a more serious trespass when the request, if honored, will reward and benefit you and so many others; the ultimate purpose of the Master's plans.

WHO IS DRIVING MY LOVE TRAIN?
A STORY OF LIFE, LOVE, AND FINDING ME

I dare to chuckle as I think about my disregard for a whispered, "Take care of yourself, Stephany." For approximately two years! And I must admit that I'm actually slightly embarrassed to share this.

Yes, my heavenly Father—who I have gotten to know so much better during these years of COVID craziness—gently suggested I do something. Yes! He told me what to do. By the way, He gently reminded me of His request more times than I want to think about. I can't justify ignoring what I know God told me to do, especially when His request was for my own benefit. So why did I need a car accident to understand what He had lovingly and repeatedly whispered to me for more than a year, "Take care of yourself. Take care of your house."

*****

"Be still and know that I am God." (Psalm 46:10 NLT)

Ironically, during this same two-year period, I confessed daily, "Lord, I am depending on you and NOT myself. Guide me. Direct me, etc. I can now almost hear Him saying, "Yeah, yeah, Stephany, and what have I told you to do?" I'm not quite certain He would speak to me like that, but that's my interpretation as I reflect back. I don't recall if He did, but I would certainly understand why He might want to. As I reflect and analyze the concept of being still, I realize that my behavior over these last two years is the antithesis of what it should have been.

I understand that the Hebrew word for still as used in Psalms 46:10, means to "sink down, relax, let go, cease striving, or withdraw." And what have I done in the last two years? 'Do, do, and do'. Aiming, instead, to be a good steward and 'do' the Grace thing, but in typical Stephany the thinker fashion. I struggled to intellectualize, understand, and differentiate spiritual biblical concepts:

How can I be a 'doer' of the Word while depending on God?
Can I literally just wait for God and lean not to my own understanding?

And, if so, how long do I wait?

Is it really just enough for me to love everybody?

Don't I at least have to remind people that God loves them?

And, if I literally depend on You, Heavenly Father, what am I supposed to do?

In the meantime, God periodically whispers, "Take care of yourself." And, by now, He's added, "And those people you continue to worry about, just love them, Stephany. Remember, I've got them."

I hear this, yet I continue to be the 'doer' that others need while squeezing in some self-care time. I've changed my diet but am still struggling a little to regularly exercise. I have lost weight but am not yet at my goal. I have even begun to explore options regarding my house. Should I sell it? Buy a new one? Explore make-over options? I bought a few home design books.

*****

"But if we look forward to something we don't yet have, we must wait patiently and confidently. (Romans 8: 25 NLT)

One night recently, I was watching a talk show. A well-known entertainer shared something he had learned from his experiences. He reflected, "I've learned that things don't happen to us. They happen for us." I remember thinking that I like that and decided to add the quote to my list of favorite quotes about life. How little did I know at the time that I'd be focusing on this concept more than I ever envisioned and so much sooner than I expected?

On Wednesday, January 4th, 2023, life as I knew it came to a screeching, grinding halt when my rally-red metallic SUV crumbled from the impact of a collision with a Jeep Wrangler. I was entering a major intersection in midtown Atlanta. With God's blessing and angels of protection, I walked away without a scratch. One look, however, at my once pretty, spiffy pride and joy reminded me of so many things. Note that I was too sad to even look at the photographic evidence taken at the accident scene, but it did not take a long time for me to realize the broader implications of the accident.

By January 5th, I realized that driving and commuting in metro Atlanta had become a major problem for me. Not quite a nightmare, though I quickly realized it had the potential to become one. One might even say that I was a little apprehensive about driving. Yes, the same lady who would hop in her SUV just to take a ride on a bright sunny day shuddered when starting up her 30-day rental car, reserving it to run errands only when absolutely necessary.

The first Sunday after the accident, I didn't have a vehicle, so I watched the service online. I knew I could not make a habit of this—not after God had literally wrapped me in His arms. So two weeks after the accident, I struggled to make my weekly 45-minute (one-way) trip to church. Fortunately, my Sunday morning playlists provided the comfort and assurance I needed. How could I listen to "Do What You are Famous For," an assurance of God's protection?

Note that I travel on the back roads these days—no interstate highway for me. I cancelled my tentative plans for a drive to New York for my sister's annual 4th of July cookout without a second thought. I haven't firmly decided yet, but my first cross-country road trip—tentatively planned for 2024—sits on the back burner. The thought of canceling it hit me as hard as the army tank look-alike Jeep Wrangler that destroyed my SUV. This trip has been on my bucket list for years. Ironically, I'd begun to research route options and develop my travel itinerary about three weeks before the accident.

My plan to be almost debt-free in eighteen months crumbled, just like my SUV's front end and my much-anticipated "burn the SUV payment book".

The analyst in me critiqued the circumstances of the accident over and over. I had just left my daughter after a relaxing day of post-holiday shopping, lunch, and chit-chat.

How could this happen? Why did this happen? And finally, I ask, "Lord, what am I to learn from this situation?"

I continued to pray about this for several weeks; forcing myself to drive - anxious, tense, unsure, but refusing to succumb to the thought that I'd lost my love of driving. More importantly, I knew my accident had to have a bigger message and meaning for me.

*****

"So use your whole body as an instrument to do what is right for the glory of God." Romans 6:13 (NLT).

"And by the way, Stephany, while you've been anxiously looking for something to 'do', I gave you two assignments."

It's funny because, in my one-on-one dialogues with the Lord, I never detect an accusatory tone. So, this time, I didn't question what I already knew. The Lord relayed His message to me two years or so ago and again periodically throughout this period. The message came so regularly and clearly that I shared His personal message to me with my children and one of my sisters. Interestingly, none of them challenged the revelation that I shared with them. They'd either nod as though in agreement or actually offer comments of their own…

"Yes, you do need to take care of yourself. Or, "Yes, you deserve a break."

WHO IS DRIVING MY LOVE TRAIN?
A STORY OF LIFE, LOVE, AND FINDING ME

In retrospect, I now know what God already knew. How can He use me, if I am not physically and mentally ready? How could I become a living instrument?

*****

"We now have this light shining in our hearts, but we ourselves are like fragile clay jars containing this great treasure. [a] This makes it clear that our great power is from God, not from ourselves. 2nd Corinthians 4:7 (NLT)

How could I forget that He is the Potter? Not only am I His instrument, I've forgotten that He has to "mold me and make me" in order for me to become the instrument He wants me to be.

And I finally realize that my doing mindset, for now, must be premised on my acceptance that His leading and guiding me during this period means that I need to stand still. If I'm not hearing "do and go", I stand still. God has the responsibility to guide and direct me to be the person He wants me to be in order to do what He wants me to do.

*****

Passing my Finding Me Exam

1. *Get to know Him.* Read. Study. Pray. God is driving my Love Train.
2. *Live a yielded life.* Accept that my qualifications to do anything and everything require my dependence on God. His power. Not my skills and self-sufficiency.
3. *Wait on Him.* I'm the passenger. My train leaves the station when He's ready. And it will not depart without me.
4. *He will instruct and teach me.* Desire and work for His good pleasure.

*****

So, here are a few tips on what you can do your season of waiting:

Pray and ask God about the purpose of this season of waiting.

Practice what you learned in the previous season.

Focus on the now.

Take this opportunity to grow closer to God.

Be content with your season and trust God's timing...Get your attitude right.

Chapter 3

When the World Conspired Against Her... She Survived

by Miracle C. Austin

Learning to love yourself without the outside influences of others can be a challenging but empowering process. As a teenage mother, it was even more difficult, as I was growing up with family influences. It's essential to prioritize your own physical and emotional well-being. Find ways to take care of yourself, such as relaxing, walking, or spending time with friends who support and encourage you. While it's essential to learn to love your life without the outside influences of others, surrounding yourself with positive and supportive people can be helpful. Take some time to reflect on what self-love means to you and how it can help you to love your life without the influence of others. It can be easy to focus on what you don't have or haven't accomplished, but it's important to focus on your strengths and achievements. Connect with people who inspire and uplift you, whether it's friends, family, or mentors.

Many of us grow up without knowing ourselves and where we want to go in life. We have different influences that help mold us into becoming who we aspire to be. We have our parents, siblings, extended family members, friends, church, and school, and you get my point. You think one way, but then you're challenged by others to see things in a different lite. You walk on one path, but someone tells you that you should walk in a different direction. That is the era I grew up in.

Teenage mothers have it hard because they are told they are too young to know what they're doing. Some families want to continue to be fully involved in assisting you. Then some families are hands-off, not around but still trying to influence your life. You're ready to be on your own and know what that looks like, but everyone else wants to have their hands on your future. If you are a teenager with a child, attending college, and working a job, you still need family support. We were forced to get jobs, go to school, and keep our children, all at the same time. You begin doing things independently, learning as you go, and figuring things out. I moved out first, and then my husband moved in. We made it with the grace of God and with lots of prayers and hard work. We did it our way, and although it may not have been the best, we figured out how to kickstart our lives for the best of our immediate family.

WHEN THE WORLD CONSPIRED AGAINST HER...SHE SURVIVED

My journey would take me from New Jersey to Georgia, to California, and back to Georgia, where we live today. Growing up, I thought New Jersey and New York would be the only places I would reside. No one could ever tell me that I would end up being a Georgia peach! I had a few travels to other states, but nowhere I wanted to set my sites on permanently, or so I thought at the time. Once I graduated from high school, my mom convinced me to move to Georgia. My grandmother was in New Jersey at the time, raising me. However, I realized I missed my mother. Once I arrived in Georgia, I began to think this was the wrong decision for my son and me. I no longer had the support I had in New Jersey, with my extended family babysitting and helping me raise my son. This was one of many bad decisions to come when I didn't think on my own. Little did I know GOD had other plans for me, and had I not prayed and listened, I would not have met the man of my dreams.

Influencers today are different from the era I grew up in. Today's influencers come in various forms, such as social media, television, and radio, which have built a platform for others to follow. This is the new era where influencers can be exotic dancers today and a guest at the White House tomorrow. The constant exposure to filtered and edited content has created unrealistic expectations and a distorted sense of reality. We are bombarded with messages that tell us what we should wear, what we should look like, and how we should behave. It is easy for us to get caught up in the race for likes and followers, but it is essential to remember that these external success measures do not matter. We must be encouraged to follow our path and seek God's guidance. We must not forget that we have unique talents and passions that are gifts from God, and we should use them to impact the world positively. Social media can have a significant impact on our behavior and beliefs. By instilling a sense of purpose and a strong moral compass, we can navigate through the influences caused by social media and stay true to ourselves.

In life, we have always been consumed with what others think we should or should not do. As I walked through life growing our family, we had all types of challenges. Outside influencers were trying to give input on how to structure our family. This was more evident when we decided to purchase a home. We had a family member telling us what and where we should buy. Other family members told us how much house we could afford without knowing our finances. Even though we wanted moral support from our family, we quickly realized we knew what best fit our own family. Now, imagine someone telling you what you should be doing in your household. Would you let your family members or friends tell you how and when to purchase something with your money? Imagine how fulfilling it is to make your own decisions. Those are some issues relationships have from the beginning until the end. Sometimes it can be the end of a relationship or marriage.

I remember when my son got a mole removed from his chin. A few of our family members told us that it was his beauty mark and that God put that there, so we should not remove it. The family did not know this bothered him because kids made fun of him. We sought medical advice and were told that there was a possibility that it could turn into a cancerous mole one day. Once we heard there was any chance of it becoming cancerous, we immediately decided to have it removed. Our families only wanted to influence our decision not to remove it, based on their upbringing. This is an example of generational influences. Each generation tends to have a unique experience that shapes their views. Always follow your instincts and do what's best for you and your family.

Relationships can sometimes be challenging; both partners must be on the same page. One partner may still want outside influencers to help them with decision-making. In contrast, the other partner wants the decision-making to be made between the two of them. Something that can seem so simple - like deciding if you should have a large and expensive wedding versus a small, inexpensive, intimate wedding -can create so much havoc with outside influence. My husband and I decided not to listen to others, and we had that small, affordable wedding. One, we wanted to avoid getting a loan or going into credit card debt for our wedding, and then having to pay for it over a long period. Of course, we had family members who wanted us to have that large church wedding with all the bells and whistles. Yet here we stand after decades of marriage. On the other hand, some family members are still paying for those wedding bills and are divorced now. Their marriage didn't last as long as the payments for their wedding.

We grow up getting the knowledge we need to leave and fly independently. You no longer want parental influence in your life. For some, that may be okay. For others, you are probably saying, not me, no way! I say to you, enjoy all the drama that comes with that advice. You must be careful when you use the advice given. That's what they call these outside influencers, advisors. Now, there is good advice and bad advice. Some people listen to you and let you form your own opinion, while others want to tell you how to solve your problem. I may have lost you in this lesson, but the lesson here is following your own lead! Remember, you may still be paying for that beautiful expensive wedding everyone influenced you to have. Now you are divorced, still have those wedding bills, and vow you'll never get married again.

You will learn, grow and find your true self without all the influencers and advice. You will learn how to survive on your own because, let's face it, the older generation - those influencers who raised you - will not be on this earth forever to support you. As you walk with your partner hand in hand, you will discover that you only need each other's support. However, now that you have been doing your own thing without outside influences, some will wonder how and why you cut everyone off. You tell them that you did not cut anyone out of your life. You cut out the noise and drama. You now make your own decisions. Communicating is the key, but comprehension must be shared in the experience. Those are powerful things to have in your relationship: communication, planning, and goals. You influence each other, becoming one in your decisions.

Some influencers may only sometimes have positive input, and some will tell you that you will fail and won't be successful. As a teenage mom, I was told by some influencers that I would have several kids before the age of 20, be on government assistance, have a regular job, and not survive in this world without family help. Without faith and belief in myself, I would not have survived. You truly must have faith in God and follow your own path so you can learn to survive in this world. When you pray on it and ask for God's direction, you don't have to worry about listening to others' advice. My mistakes and the horrible things that happened to me in my younger years would not defeat me. Those influencers – and their predictions of what I would be - triggered me into survival mode. This was the last time I listened to anyone other than myself and God.

"No Weapon Formed Against You Shall Prosper." Isaiah 54:17

Has an influencer ever caused you to make a life-changing decision? We weren't happy in Atlanta. Other family members influenced us to move to California. Never give other people the power to make your life-changing decisions. My husband had been given a scholarship to play football, and I also had family there. I could attend college. This turned out to be a bad decision, being put out of a family's home with nowhere to go and not wanting to leave your loved one behind. Be patient; sometimes, you must endure the worst to get to the best. My husband was working part-time, and we shared about $250 a week, plus he had school and played football. No money, no real job, and in one of the most expensive states. Sometimes, God takes you on a journey you didn't know you needed to bring you everything you ever wanted. Trust the plan, no matter how it appears at the time.

Moving back to Atlanta was eventually the best thing for us. We were both back at home with our mothers, which lasted a month or two. You can't hear God's voice because you are listening to other voices. Once again, we had to shut everyone out to walk our own journey. We began our own path and set our goals and sights on the best we could obtain in life. We went from apartment to apartment several times before finally renting and then purchasing our first home. We always had cars; my husband is a car guy. They were constantly maintained so that we could get to work. We began working at Wendy's in our early years and ended up working for some of the largest corporations in the world. We later finished college and built small businesses along with our continued nine-to-five jobs. We finally did it all our way, and oh, what a blessing it has been. We learned to have goals and a budget and complete our dreams. We still have that same desire and strategy to win.

Setting goals is a critical factor in achieving success and fulfillment in life, but there are other important aspects to consider. Setting goals for yourself can help you to focus on the present and the future rather than dwelling on the past or what others think of you. Take responsibility for your success; do not rely on others to make things happen. One of the most significant parts of making it in life without being heavily influenced by external factors is developing a strong sense of self-awareness and self-discipline. Stay focused and committed to your goals despite distractions or obstacles. We've fallen out of focus plenty of times, wanting that new car, going on a shopping spree, going on vacation, and just wanting everything now because we can afford to. You must have a strong sense of purpose and a willingness to put in the hard work and dedication necessary to achieve your goals.

As we focused on ourselves and what we wanted to accomplish, we built our own lives from the ground up. We failed at some things, and we won at others. We sometimes must make things work on our own because we shut out those outside influences, strengthening our bond. Once we focused on ourselves and began to reach for the goals we wanted to achieve, we watched our life flourish abundantly. We raised our children and allowed them to be the best and be in a great position to begin their own journey. Now we see the fruits of our labor with our grandchildren following in our footsteps and reaching for it all while loving their lives without outside influences. This must be taught to them because if you don't teach it, they can become what you ultimately tried to avoid. As a parent, it is easy to do when you want so much for your offspring. As a mom, I cannot say I have been perfect at it because I sometimes try to influence the outcome when one has gone astray. Luckily, I have the other half of me remind me, and I do the same for him. You see, it is easy to have outside influences that sometimes want to help, but they also can overstep the boundaries and take over. This is a lesson that can be a generational problem if not realized.

Some outside influences can be guides. We have some best friends that are just that. They sit back and listen and do not try to influence us. They also are the same friends that we sit back and listen to when they need us. Just imagine two couples loving life and building their families but also being able to have different life experiences. They uplift us when we're down so we can share our innermost feelings and not be judged by any decisions. We have those positive and supportive people in our life and cherish them. We have been broken together at one point or another. We have been on top of our game at one point or another. We have had issues with our children falling off track at some time or another. Today we vacation together and talk about how far we have come, how our lives were, and where they are now. Our self-care is traveling the world with our lifelong friends until we have seen it all. We are living our best lives without outside influences.

Influencers tell you that you need to get out more and hang out. Set boundaries and be firm and clear about your boundaries and why they are important to you. You will have things you want to do that your partner doesn't. How do you accomplish that? Communicate with them regularly about how you're feeling and what your needs are. Practicing self-care in a relationship can be challenging, especially if others influence you to spend more time with them. Remember that self-care is a process, and making mistakes is okay. As you mature, the club scene no longer grabs your attention. I remember dying to go to a club, but it was less desirable as I evolved. You learn that you make your own scene, which isn't necessarily hanging out in the club. There is a time and a place for that to occur, and those same scenes will be there whenever you want them. Remember, learning to love yourself without the outside influences of others is a journey, and it may not happen overnight. Be patient with yourself and take small steps each day to build self-love and confidence.

Your past is your past, and it made you who you are. You have no regrets and wouldn't change a thing. You don't have to live in it anymore! As you watch your children grow and flourish, you'll know that you have defied the odds and surpassed the expectations set by society. You will have created a beautiful life for yourself and your family through sheer determination and unwavering love. Now you'll take pride in teaching your grandchildren how to navigate through this world without having too many outside influences take over. You'll teach them how to come into themselves and be their best selves for them. You will have proven that it was possible to succeed despite the challenges and hardships that life may have thrown your way. As you reflect on your journey, you'll smile with pride, knowing you survived and thrived against all odds.

"The Lord is my Strength and my Shield," Psalm 28:7

Chapter 4

Make Yourself Known

by Lisa R. Robinson Patterson

Making yourself known…how do I begin!? I got married at 21, and after 40 years, we have 6 adult children.

Everything was happening so fast – motherhood, new wife – there was no time to figure out what I wanted to do in life. I had an idea of what I wanted to become, but I wondered if I would fulfill my dreams.

God already knew what He had in store for my daily life. Often, as women, we're not sure where to start a career, or when. Some choose a career first, then marriage and children. Our plates stay full of daily needs from all sides of life, keeping it all together from sunrise to sunset. As a wife and mother, our desires are put on hold to focus on family. We start each new day with a schedule that quickly changes. More things get added than taken away. We find comfort in little things – a husband's kiss or a child's hug.

I pray to the Lord for guidance and strength. As a Christian getting to know my journey, I know that the Lord has a plan for my life, so I need to take time for Him. He knows all about me, but do I know who I am in Him? As women, we put ourselves on a shelf, under a pillow, or in a closet. There's no time for ourselves, but we need to make time where we can. Maybe a moment for relaxation or even a nap.

I tried to work outside the home, but finding babysitters was not easy. Then, my child began to cry when I tried to leave, so I then became a stay-at-home mother. My daily tasks consisted of getting kids ready for school, cleaning, cooking, and washing clothes, and everything else that comes with motherhood and homemaking.

The Lord gives us talents. We think, "Where did that come from?" Jesus put it there! As women, sometimes we cannot see the potential in ourselves, but others can. Our eyes can be blinded and our ears clogged. It may take years to find our purpose. We need to trust and have faith in God. So, unlock those closets and uncover that blanket from your head. The Lord's presence is ALL about His light! So, let us shine! Make yourself known! My walk through the years as a wife and mother of six has been a journey.

After the kids were older and began to take on some responsibilities, I decided to start the career I dreamed of. I worked for fifteen years and have now retired, but I have not done it all. I do not think God intended for us to do it all. Take one day at a time to make yourself known. Even though I worked in and outside the home, all I knew was home.

As women, we do what we've been taught by our mothers, grandmothers, and aunts from generation to generation. Unfortunately, some women don't have a female relative to teach us. What about you (me)? Make yourself known! Many women only let a little light shine, afraid to let their full light be seen or known. It's easy to wonder what others may say – suppressing our feelings. It's easy to put ourselves down, to think we're not good enough. But that is so far from the truth!

Do everything for the glory of God! He loves YOU the most. Make yourself known! I've learned that I need to make more of myself known to God every moment of my life. He made Himself known to me as soon as I accepted Him in my life. "No, in all these things we are more than conquerors through Him who loved us." (Romans 8:37) NIV

I am more than a conqueror through Christ Jesus my Lord. So why am I hiding who He has created me to be? I am 60 years old, retired, trying to figure out what and where to go from here. I feel that I've spent my life thinking about everyone and everything else, and rarely about myself. Make yourself known!

We can lose ourselves through lack of rest, not eating properly, stress, not accepting our appearance, and not focusing on our walk with the Lord. The emotional pain that comes when we lose ourselves is real. How did this happen, and why? I let this go on for so long. I thought I had control. I let stuff slip in, trying to fix brokenness in my mind, body, and spirit. We beat ourselves too much. Thank God for how He has brought you (me) out once again and again. Jesus knows who you are and what you can do. Take time with Him and it will be revealed unto you.

We want to be accepted and praised for what we have done and are doing. It is a daily struggle, and so many blocked views get in the way. I need God to lead me. The path seems lonely at times, but God has been there with me ALL along!

Find your comfort zone and something you like to do. In my life, I've been told I should do this or that. But I wasn't sure of what I wanted to do. My first love is sewing. I've found that doing puzzles is relaxing. I like to draw and paint. There is a purpose for what we do. It is all for HIS glory. Those are talents that God has given me. I should be proud of myself and my talents! I've begun to make myself known to others, but I am still hiding behind my talents.

We make excuses every day. There's no time. There's nothing to wear. My hair's not done. The house is a mess. The list goes on and on. Stop making excuses for her (you)!

Many of us want approval for our appearance and actions. There are so many expectations in life. We feel that other people judge our appearance, from our hair to our toes, so we want to look beautiful. But inside, we feel miserable, ugly, and lonely. I know that other people see beauty in me, but when I look in the mirror, sometimes I only see hurt, tears, shame, weakness, and stress. The weight of all the perceived faults can damage the mind and body. You may have low self-esteem that can leave scars for a long time. Encourage yourself! Gradually move yourself to a better place. I am trying to do this myself. I need to encourage myself, tell myself that I can do it! No one's approval matters by mine and God's!

When you feel it is right in your spirit, then it is totally alright with God. When we truly walk and trust His Word, the Lord will reveal what He has planned for you.

"For I know the plans I have for you, declares the Lord, plans to prosper you and not to harm you, plans to give you hope and a future." (Jeremiah 29:11) NIV

Whatever makes you feel beautiful, do it! "Your beauty should not come from outward adornment, such as braided hair and the wearing of gold jewelry and fine clothes. Instead, it should be that of your inner self, the unfading beauty of a gentle and quiet spirit, which is of great worth in God's sight." (I Peter 3:3-4) NIV

The joy of the Lord can erase all scars. We as women need to put God's grace back into our lives and live according to His Word on beauty. There is beauty in Jesus and His creation. He created me to be "me" and you to be "you". We are His daughters.

I may not be what or who the world perceives me to be, but this is who I am right now, at this moment in my life. I am going to be just fine! Allow the Lord to give you peace, instead of accepting the pain that wants to destroy you.

We are people-pleasers. We try to make everyone happy and meet their needs. In doing this, we place our needs on hold. Don't wait for others to meet your needs; they can't do that if they don't know what they are. We must focus on our own emotional, mental, and physical health and stop allowing all the "stuff" to affect our lives. Every day, the Lord gives us is another day to breathe, to see, to walk, and to speak. He will help you overcome the pain you see in the mirror. But he can only help you if you start making a change in the way you see the world – and yourself. It is a daily task. Keep telling yourself "I can do this. I am embracing my inner and outer beauty. What God has for you is for you. I see you changing. I feel you getting stronger."

First, it starts with you and Jesus allowing you to get where you want to be. There is no you without the Lord! You need Him! You cannot do life by yourself. He knows all about you. Now, allow God to bring forth what He has created you to be. MAKE YOURSELF KNOWN!

Beginning to Know Myself

When I was asked to include part of my life in Part 2 of the book, Who's Sleeping with My Husband, I immediately felt that I could not do it. I continued to think on it and pray, asking for God's help. I wanted to share what would be of most help to women who read the book. Hindrances and roadblocks came from all directions, but I made up my mind that I could do it. As I began to write my journey, I realized that my life does count, and I have done more than I imagined!

As a school bus driver, I touched many young people's lives, from discipline to encouragement. I spoke to a student on my bus who stayed in trouble. I saw him a few years later and he told me his behavior had gotten better. I said, "I knew you could do it!" I am thankful for the opportunity to encourage him.

I have made sewing projects from measurements and mailed them to customers. I altered a prom dress from a size 10 to a size 4. Even though I thought I would burn out and not complete it, I did it! The mother and daughter were pleased, and I received extra pay. Over ten years ago, I made curtains by measurements for my sister-in-law's mother. I was very proud of those curtains, and still am. The mother is now deceased, but the curtains remain in the home.

I have been blessed during my time as a caregiver to the elderly and those in need. I am beginning to know myself! I am also discovering my God-given talents through decorating, painting, and doing crafts. I have been praying about how to best share these talents. I give many of my creations away, but I'm considering starting a business to sell them if it is the will of God. Self-worth has begun to surface!

MAKE YOURSELF KNOWN

Realizing your value and worth makes a difference. You can uncover yourself from that blanket, or open the closet door, and stop hiding. Instead of the disappointing image in the mirror, you can look at the reflection and see the beauty God has given you. Your blind eyes will be opened, and the scales will be gone. There will be no more tears to run your mascara. The tissue box will remain full! Take off the garments of heaviness and let God place a robe of joy and peace upon you. BEGIN NOW TO MAKE YOUR SELF KNOWN!

Chapter 5

Who Are You?
Who's Sleeping With
Your Husband?

by Jolie Rashawn

WHO'S SLEEPING WITH YOUR HUSBAND TOO?

Whew! The Title of the chapter had you gasping for air, didn't it? Yeah, it got me too. But when I really stop and think about it, it's a damn good question.

Who is sleeping with my husband? It seems like an easy question to answer because we look at it from the point of view of an outside woman coming in and sleeping with something that's already mine. What if I told you that your first thought isn't what the question is asking. So, let me ask it again, who is sleeping with your husband, too?

When I really sat down and thought about this, the real question I had to ask; Jolie, who are you? I had to really sit and realize that the question is pertaining to me and who I am, and who I have been portraying all this time.

My husband is sleeping with the inner little girl in me who was hurt years ago by someone she trusted. Who was stripped of her innocence, and her femininity and never fully recovered from it. The little girl who would never truly know what the true definition of love is, and who would lose out on being in a position to learn who she is, and the things that she loves to do, she would never be in a place to be normal like other little girls would. She would never not know the desire of a man because it was forced on her. My husband is sleeping with a broken little girl who is screaming for help to find her true identity.

My husband is sleeping with this young teenage girl who would allow people to mentally manipulate her into thinking she wasn't good enough, or that she didn't belong in groups, or in clubs at school, and the dance hall that we had in our city. All it took was for one or two people not to believe in her, and it gave her the push to not believe in herself either. If someone said she was dumb, she figured maybe they were right because they knew better than her.

My husband is sleeping with this young teenage girl that in spite of all of the things that she had been going through, they must have known something she didn't, so she went along with whatever was thrown at her, and she started to really see that she had no self-identity at all. She was living for the masses. It was sad and hurtful, but she felt like this was her life and the way it was always going to be, and she was learning to cope and deal with it.

My husband is sleeping with the young teenage girl who has taken on the identity of so many different people, because she is too embarrassed to come into her own identity. She has lost all confidence in herself, and at this point will do whatever she is told to feel accepted.

This young girl, that my husband is sleeping with is crying out because she doesn't know why her body is reacting to pleasures and desires of the mind, of things in her mind that should not be there. This young teenage girl that my husband is sleeping with knows all too well what it feels like to masturbate and to desire a man's touch, to desire his lips and his tongue over her body. This young teenage girl is fantasizing of any man and his private parts, rubbing and touching against hers. This teenage girl that my husband is sleeping is now thinking of ways to seduce men, and to give herself to any man who will show her some attention because that's all she knows. This teenage girl that my husband is sleeping with is in a dangerous position because she has no identity of her own, and she is fully vulnerable to anyone who comes along.

My husband is sleeping with the teenage young lady who has fully had the taste of a man and is now in full crave mode for more. She is like a vampire in need of blood to survive, but this young teenage lady that my husband is sleeping with has now created a void that can never be filled. It doesn't matter how many men she sleeps with it doesn't matter how many men she practices her sexual acts on to be sure she's ready for the next man. The void is never filled. It doesn't matter how many men she seduces and causes to cheat on their wives. The void is not filled. It doesn't matter how many threesomes this young woman has; the void is still not filled. And although she doesn't know that the more sex she has, the bigger and deeper the black hole gets. This young teenage woman that my husband is sleeping with has now begun what should be an embarrassing track record for herself; it is now becoming her checklist to see just how close or far off she is from feeling this massive sexual appetite.

This young lady that my husband is sleeping with is now part of the statistics. She is a young African American single mother, who is still in high school, and has now "ruined her life" as the world puts it, because she had plans to go and play basketball, to go to school for nursing. This young lady who had all of these dreams and aspirations is now seeing that none of these will be fulfilled because she has now made decisions that are changing her life. This young lady that my husband is sleeping with does not understand why this is happening to her. She is not understanding why no one loves her, or why every man that comes into her is not sticking around for the long haul. You see, this young lady that my husband is sleeping with was told in the beginning that she was beautiful. That she was loved. She was told that she was the favorite. She was told and made to feel like she was the only one that was important. But once the nookie was taken, and the dust settled, this young lady that my husband is sleeping with realized that every man was singing the same tune. This young lady that my husband is sleeping with, her track record is growing immensely, and it is becoming normal for her to want more and more of a man regardless of how he treats her, what he says to her, the lies he tells. It didn't matter to her because all this young lady that my husband is sleeping with knew was that a man coming into her was the best feeling ever, and if she could experience more of it and more pleasure from it and different men and different sizes in different positions and different connections, that maybe her void would be filled.

This lady that my husband is sleeping with is now a high school graduate, but she is also a single mother of two children, and she is in an abusive relationship. This lady that my husband is sleeping with does not know how to stand up for herself; in fact, she is extremely weak. This lady that my husband is sleeping with has no voice, and it doesn't matter how much she attempts to stand up for herself. None of it is working. The more she stands up, the more she is knocked down. The more she attempts to try and move around and make things better, the more she is reminded that she is worthless. The more this lady that is sleeping with my husband tries to make a name for herself, the more she is reminded that nobody will want her.

She is reminded that she's damaged goods. She is reminded that life is over for her. This lady that my husband is sleeping with is in an emotional, verbal, and physically abusive relationship, and now she has four small children to take care of.

This lady that my husband is sleeping with is so beautiful, but she will never see it looking through the lenses that she has. She will only see the beauty of others, and she will never see the work that God has placed on the inside of her. This lady that my husband is sleeping with is so broken and so bruised and she has given up on life as she thought she knew it. She has given up on someone loving her. She has given up on the possibility of a family.

This lady that my husband is sleeping with has been stripped of everything she had. She has been on housing, and she has been trying to work, she had a car, and she was doing well for herself. In the midst of that, she lost her housing, she lost her job, and she lost her car.

This lady that my husband is sleeping with is now homeless with three of her small children. She is having to sleep in parks with her children, wondering if they are going to make it through the night, wondering if something will happen to them if she falls asleep, wondering if things ever get better for them.

This lady that my husband is sleeping with has begun to blame herself for everything. Looking at her children; suffering broke her spirits more than anything. This lady that my husband is sleeping with is now having to ride the bus with her children and seek out different churches that have shelters to try and provide some sort of roof over their head. And although sometimes it is successful, it still is not safe.

This lady that my husband is sleeping with has reached rock -bottom, and she knows that the only way to go from here is up. But nobody is sending her a lifeline or a rope or a ladder to help her out of the hole she is in. This lady that my husband is sleeping with has no friends, so she thinks, to help her. One day, a lifeline comes and she is able to come off the streets with her children and stay in a warm home. And although it is temporary, it is necessary for her journey. It is necessary to start the rebuilding of her life.

This lady that my husband is sleeping with is now on marriage number two, and honey let me tell you the man that she has if I may be frank, he ain't shit! The lady that my husband is sleeping with is settling for a man who does not work, who is living off of her. This man that she's married to is sleeping with all types of women and having children with them while she is still in the home, making sure that there is a roof over their head, that there are vehicles to drive, and there are phones for communication. She is making sure that all bills are being paid as well as money in his pocket This lady that my husband is sleeping with is making sure that there are hot meals on the table for dinner and that the man she's married to never has to want for anything. This lady that my husband is sleeping with is settling for a good piece of meat to satisfy her at night, and in her mind, that's enough. This lady that my husband is sleeping with is embarrassed beyond to say that she has someone there she is willing to put up with everything that's going on. The lady that my husband is sleeping with puts up with this for seven years and after he gets tired of dealing with her, he leaves her and never returns.

This lady that my husband is sleeping with is now developing anxiety and depression, and she does not know how to control it, because the events leading up to where she is having been so traumatic that now all of that suppressed pressure is bursting like pipes. This lady that my husband is sleeping with is now contemplating things to do to herself.

This lady that my husband is sleeping with no longer wants to live. She is thinking that maybe life would be better without her, maybe her children would be better off without her. The woman that my husband is sleeping with has become numb to life itself. She has begun to depend on medications to sedate her, and she's only there to take her children to and from school. Everything else in her life means nothing. The lady that my husband is sleeping with has grown to be more and more bitter. So now, she is targeting men for the things that all of the men in her life have taken from her.

The lady that my husband is sleeping with is dangerous! She does not value life, not even her own, and she does not care about putting her life in harm's way. She is at the point where she will take whatever it is that she wants. She is determined to get what she wants, and she does not mind ruining the lives of men to have it.

This lady that my husband is sleeping with does not value marriage, she does not value relationships, and she does not value love. This lady that my husband is sleeping with, is out for revenge. Not so much on the ones who were responsible for the things that were done to her, but revenge on the male species in general. Any man that encounters her, she devours them like a roaring lion. It is almost as if it would be better for him not to notice her, because in her eyes, everyone is guilty, and she is on a mission to punish every man that got in her path. This lady that my husband is sleeping with, has miraculously found God and has begun to get closer and closer to him. This lady has found an outlet, modeling, which has begun to rebuild her confidence. She is rebuilding her self-esteem, and she is realizing that there is more to her than what she had noticed over her entire life. This lady that my husband is sleeping with is really trying to take a step back from men. Trying to really find herself and her purpose.

This lady that my husband is sleeping with is starting to love things about herself. Her smile, her laughter. She is learning her favorite colors and her favorite foods. She is learning why she likes some things and doesn't like others. This lady that my husband is sleeping with is learning to forgive. It is a hard road at this point but it is very necessary. This lady that is sleeping with my husband, she knows that it's necessary to get there. This lady that is sleeping with my husband has become happier and more outgoing in her life. She is coming to terms with being alone and accepting the "what if" possibilities.

The lady that my husband is sleeping with is making a name for herself: Jolie Rashawn! She is making a name for herself that people have grown to know and love. This lady that is sleeping with my husband never forgot where she began; she has made sure to remember her humble beginnings. She remembers the bad, but she has begun to congratulate herself for her small victories. This lady that my husband is sleeping with is so smart and she has a heart of gold, and she will give you the shirt off of her back. She would be sure that your needs come before hers. This lady that my husband is sleeping with has begun to explore new possibilities in her life. What are the things that she likes? What is it that she wants to do to better herself and those around her?

This lady that my husband is sleeping with is truly amazing.

Although it seems like the lady that my husband has been sleeping with is a past tense person, she is very much alive. You see, although the woman who my husband is sleeping with now has evolved, she is still very much the young lady, the young teenager, the little girl, who was ripped of her innocence years ago. You see, all of those make up the woman my husband is sleeping with, and without them, there would be no her.

This woman that my husband is now sleeping with loves herself unconditionally! She is unapologetic about things that have happened to her in her past, for she knows all of those have made her strong. This woman that my husband is sleeping with he is ready to speak to the masses and show the world how important it is to step in walking the truth. She shows people the importance of coming together and being able to uplift one another. This woman my husband is sleeping with does not take no for an answer. In fact, if the answer is no too many times, she will create her own solution and not have to answer to anyone. This woman that my husband is sleeping with has made her feel more secure. He has reassured her that things are going to be okay, and she believes him.

This woman that my husband is now sleeping with knows no boundaries. She is determined to succeed in every area of her life. This woman has made a name for herself, and will not allow anyone to make her feel ashamed of her past, or to make her feel inferior to anyone else. This woman who my husband is sleeping with now, when I tell you the power that she holds in her soul to make things happen, who does not mind working and seeing things through because she remembers a time when she did not have anything, and how hard she worked to show that you cannot keep her down for long. This woman has this amazing crazy faith in God, and she knows that if she can think it, then she can see it, and if she can see it, she will be able to feel it. And right now, this woman that my husband is sleeping with has a vision that is so grand, nothing can stand in the way of it becoming her reality.

Sometimes I stare in the mirror at this woman that my husband is sleeping with, and I must tell her how proud I am of her for not folding, for making a bet on herself. I'm proud of her for trusting her process and knowing that one day, she will be able to make not only herself proud, but her children and her family proud. One day a conversation she had with her grandmother about seeing herself on TV and on billboards and traveling the world would become her reality. Now, she is seeing these things manifest; she is seeing the birth of what's been inside of her all along. This woman that my husband is sleeping with now, did not become blessed because of the mistakes and the trials that she went through; however, she was blessed anyway, and God proved that it doesn't matter what decisions or what trials you go through; His promise is still his promise. He showed her that it didn't matter how things started out. He had the final say on how things were going to play out.

And so, the woman that my husband is sleeping with is Me and I am Her - Jolie Rashawn the great! That is who's sleeping with my husband.

Chapter 6

Almost Abandoned

by Deena C. M. Wingard

Most people who have ever been married have thought about leaving the marriage. Of course, there are exceptional "madly in love" people for whom leaving their mate has never crossed their mind. However, it is not cynical to believe that at some point or another, most married people will wonder, "Should I stay, or should I go?"

There are many factors to consider. Due to the magnitude of the decision, it is not a choice to be made lightly. It is, therefore, a wise person who calculates the costs before deciding to leave. Alternatively, a person who leaves abruptly is, with a few exceptions, operating foolishly.

In my first book of fiction, *Almost*, the protagonist, Balynda Brown, is in a perpetual state of marital discord. As she grows increasingly unfulfilled in her marriage and life, she realizes she must make some hard choices if she ever wants to achieve her best life. We can only wear the mask of fake happiness for so long before our inner person and soul grow weary. It is important to note, however, that the decision to stay in an unfulfilling life is, in fact, a choice.

I want to identify three main categories to carefully consider before deciding to leave your marriage.

First, Can You Financially Afford to Leave?

Times have changed for women today. Both my maternal and paternal grandmothers were stay-at-home mothers. Both raised six or more children to adulthood. These two housewives were financially dependent on their husbands and had limited options when considering living elsewhere. Your options are few when you have six kids, no job, and little work history outside the home. There were even fewer options during the '30s, '40s, and '50s. It is important to note that while options for women during that era were limited, especially for women of color, many women had to and did "make do."

Many women in the '30s, '40s, and '50s worked to care for their families financially. According to an article by Kahn Academy, women were expected to identify primarily as wives and mothers and avoid working outside the home. ("Women in the 1950s (article) I 1950s America") Yet, women comprised a large portion of the post-World War II labor force.

Despite the growing number of women in the workforce in the 1950s, women were still encouraged to stay home to care for their husbands and children and not pursue a career. This viewpoint was prevalent during the Cult of Domesticity time, when "true womanhood" "was intrinsically tied to her success in domestic pursuits such as keeping a clean house, raising pious children, and being submissive and obedient to her husband." (Wigington, Patti. "The Cult of Domesticity: Definition and History.")

Yet, as noted earlier, this portrait of "true womanhood" was not applied to women of color and immigrants. Such women were expected to work hard outside the home, which became particularly challenging if she wasn't married or didn't have a man in the house, but other mouths to feed and bodies to clothe. As such, many African American women were "excluded from the chance ever to be true paragons of domestic virtue" (Wigington).

It is unsurprising that my grandmothers and many other women could not fathom ever leaving a marriage that allowed them to display "true womanhood." Many stayed even if her husband was abusive, unfaithful, or downright unlikeable.

I recall an impactful conversation I had with my grandmother. I was an adult then, so she engaged me in a woman-to-woman discussion and shared her vulnerabilities. She shared the infidelity of my grandfather during their marriage. She talked about the various interactions she had with women who were neighbors or fellow church members, bragging about relationships they had with her husband. My grandmother replayed some of the gossip she had to endure due to her man's repeated escapades. As I traveled down memory lane with her, I welcomed the conversation, as I realized it was a rite of passage, a generational transfer of family history and wisdom.

Even though I knew my grandparents stayed married until my grandfather passed, I was surprised when she stated, "But he never left me." While she undoubtedly loved my grandfather, I am sure finances were part of why she stayed and was elated that he did as well. She no doubt witnessed the struggle of her fellow African American sisters without husbands and rationalized that her plight was better. Perhaps she exclaimed a time or two, "Half a man is better than no man at all."

Now that women have worked for the past 100 years, 46.6 percent of the workforce is female. (Zane, Matthew. "What Percentage Of The Workforce Is Female?' [2023]). Although inequities toward women are still prevalent in the workplace, the propensity for a woman to financially care for her family without the assistance of a husband has vastly improved over the years. As such, while a woman may opt to stay in a marriage because of the drastic cut in or removal of her financial status, the dire circumstances many of our grandmothers faced are now just financial setbacks and not financial ruin.

Yet, we cannot overstate the economic hardships of being a single parent. An article by *Hello Motherhood* states, "while nearly half of all single-mom families live in poverty, economic distress affects only one in 10 married families with children. Two-parent households tend to live in better neighborhoods and their children attend better schools." (Moore, Ayra. "Single-Parent Family Social Problems." [2018]) Nonetheless, A single woman can survive because it has been done many times before, despite the difficult road ahead.

Secondly, Should Kids Not Have Both Parents in The Home?
It does not require statistical studies to establish that children raised in two-parent households often fare better than single-parent households.

While we have repeatedly seen the success of many single-parent homes, such was achieved through great struggle and grit. That is not to say that two-parent households require less determination and effort, but two heads are typically better than one.

Scripture even confirms this belief by telling us that:
Two are better than one, because they have a good return for their labor: If either of them falls down, one can help the other up. But pity anyone who falls and has no one to help them up. Also, if two lie down together, they will keep warm. But how can one keep warm alone? Though one may be overpowered, two can defend themselves. A cord of three strands is not quickly broken.
Ecclesiastes 4: 9-12 NIV

In addition to the above benefits, there are many other positive reasons to sustain a two-parent household. For example, two parents can better monitor their children and more easily allow them to engage in extracurricular activities. Furthermore, research has found that "children living with two biological parents or in a blended adoptive family were healthier than children living with grandparents, single moms, or step-parents." (Moore)

Despite these findings, not all two-parent homes are healthy and happy. If a child is being reared in a dysfunctional, two-parent household, it would be better for that child not to have both parents in the home. Before I provide statistical data to support my conclusion, I will first speak from my personal experience. Both of my biological parents were present in the home during my childhood. While there were many positives, my childhood was dysfunctional. I was unaware of the term "dysfunctional" at that time. But I knew that Daddy whipping Mommy was not ordinary or necessary.

Family dysfunction can take many forms, including drug and alcohol abuse, infidelity, domestic violence, and unfaithfulness. Abuse in and of itself is multi-faceted and can come in the following ways: physical, mental, verbal, sexual, spiritual, and financial. Unfortunately, this list is not exhaustive, as abuse can proliferate nearly every facet of our lives. The presence of these detrimental evils causes a family to no longer function in a positive, loving, and productive manner. The result is the creation of mental health complications and, perhaps, death.

Death can occur in various ways and in many categories. For example, physical abuse can and has often led to the loss of life. Physical abuse can also lead to the death of hopes, dreams, and ambitions. Likewise, infidelity can result in the death of a marriage and scar the witnessing children well into adulthood.

In an article by *Psychology Today*, children from dysfunctional homes are more likely to smoke cigarettes, be promiscuous, be depressed, or become an alcoholic, just to name a few (Welss, Robert. "How Adverse Childhood Experiences Affect You As An Adult." [2019]). It is also important to note that such defective behaviors can cause physical ailments like heart disease, diabetes, and hypertension. Interestingly, these diseases are disproportionately present among people of color and impoverished areas. While family dysfunction is present across all socioeconomic classes and impacts all ethnicities and demographics, there is a link between family dysfunction, poverty, and people of color. And the cycle continues unless intentionally broken.

The perpetual continuation of family dysfunction is a generational curse. If each subsequent generation continues based on their childhood experiences, the next generation will likely do the same. It takes an intentional decision not to do the same thing as your parents or other caregivers and break generational curses. Instead of operating based on habit, you must decide to do better and act differently in areas that only serve to keep one bound and headed for destruction.

Thus, if your marriage is dysfunctional and you have made efforts to remove or eliminate the harm but to no avail, you must take action.

You can pray all day and night, but if the situation has not improved and it is causing trauma to you and any children in the home, which it undoubtedly will, it is time to make an exit plan. James, in the Bible, said it best, "Faith without works is dead" (James 2:17). This leads to our third category to carefully consider before deciding to leave your marriage:

What Does God Say About Leaving Your Marriage?

I hope my traditional-thinking Christians have stayed tuned and are still reading along. If you are, I am so glad you kept reading, but I am sure you have been thinking, "What does God say about all this"? If you believe God wants us to stay married no matter what, this is especially for you.

Yes, we know that God loves marriage and hates divorce. Yet, if we look closer at Malachi 2:16, we see that the Lord stated this because the men were faithless and were discarding the wives of their youth for other (likely younger) wives. Thus, God hates divorce herein because the women were being mistreated and set aside contrary to the marital covenants. Although this scripture is often used to make the woman stay in abusive marriages, it actually supports how precious women are in God's sight. Malachi 2:16 goes on to tell us, "...To divorce your wife is to overwhelm her with cruelty," says the LORD of Heaven's Armies. "So guard your heart; do not be unfaithful to your wife." The Bible also reminds us that we are fearfully and wonderfully made (Psalms 139:14). God has masterfully crafted each one of us. Therefore, we are all unique and important in God's sight. Just think of something you took the time to create. Perhaps you have cultivated and cared for a work of art or even a plant. The Bible even uses the analogy of an earthly mother or father's love for his or her children. If you love these things, how much more does the Creator of Everything adore you?

When you love and adore something, what do you do? You care for it. You do not want it to be in hurtful situations. You want the best for that you love. God desires the same for us. Be it a man or a woman, God wants the best for us all. Therefore, God is not pleased if you live in cruel conditions and are mistreated by the person who has made a covenant to love you. God is a God of love, and because God loves us, God's permissive will allows us to free ourselves from abusive relationships.

Satan himself contorted the scripture to suit his evil devices. Surely it should come as no surprise that unrighteous people have done the same since the beginning of time. The Word of God has been contorted to keep women from preaching, enslaved Africans from trying to escape, and women from leaving abusive marriages, to name a few.

What does God say about leaving your marriage? God says, "I have come to set the captives free" (Luke 4:18). You cannot be free if the daily infliction of emotional and spiritual turmoil binds up your spirit. How can you walk worthy in the vocation wherewith you were called (Ephesians 4:1) if you are in survival mode every day and struggling to have joy? It is difficult to operate in your spiritual gifts and be all God has called you to be when the enemy has you bound.

But thanks be to God, who gives us the victory through our Lord Jesus Christ (I Corinthians 15:57)! You do not have to stay in an abusive relationship. I implore you to break the generational curses of family dysfunction and start a new family description. God has given each one of us gifts, talents, and abilities to be used to upbuild the Kingdom of God. Walking worthy is challenging with a foot on your neck, shackles on your feet, a shattered heart, and a confused mind.

Walking worthy is so difficult if you are in a dark situation that you may be tempted to abandon yourself. You may become so accustomed to being treated like less than a child of God that it becomes routine. People abused as children often grow up to become abused adults. For some, the natural tendency is to accept the abuse as your lot in life and live within those circumstances.

ALMOST ABANDONED

I am grateful that despite my history of painful relationships, I ultimately learned that God wanted better for me. I now recognize that my childhood was the product of unbroken generational curses. Most importantly, I now fully grasp that I am the aroma of Christ and, as such, refuse to be mistreated. As I have learned, I strive to be that family history changer and stop the perpetual evils the enemy brings.

I almost abandoned myself. I almost thought misery would be my lifelong companion. I pray that you receive the same revelation and begin your walk in the newness of life.

Chapter 1

Self-Love Journey: How to Start to Love by Dating Yourself

by Alexandra Sanders

All my life, I've relied on others to make me feel special. I grew up an only child, so I received a lot of my family's attention. That created an unhealthy practice of looking outward for praise and, ultimately, love. As a result, I found myself time and time again disappointed when a partner didn't give me what only I knew I needed. It became a true reality that I needed to get right with myself when I felt alone in my marriage.

It all started with my love of art galleries. Man, did I love art...so much that I'd travel far and wide to see exhibits. My husband, unfortunately, did not enjoy art as much as I did, and I took it personally. I felt that if we weren't interested in the same things, there were aspects of me that were being ignored and neglected. The reality is that not all people like the same things, and to force your partner into activities isn't sustainable nor healthy. My mistake was ignoring my own wants and blaming my partner for something I could have made special just for me. To expand further, for a good part of our relationship, I slowly fell into his shadow and forgot what I enjoyed doing. I started to pick up his hobbies, we hung around with his friends, and our quality time was spent doing things only he was passionate about.

But where was I? As a young woman I had interests, but I became resentful that I created this reality for myself all in the name of trying to be a good wife. I was a wife who was interested opposed to interesting, a wife that was supportive but essentially alone in the marriage. So, I finally made the decision to start doing things differently. I refused to feel ignored and alone. I dedicated the next several years to figuring out who Alex really was. This journey I had taken and the relationship I continue to nurture with myself to this day is a story worth sharing with other people. We're all on this journey to better understand ourselves and find new ways to fall back in love with ourselves. So, you may ask: where can I start? Date yourself...

The concept of falling in love with yourself always felt like a cliché to me until I was faced with the reality that you cannot receive or depend on love without an understanding that you are worthy of healthy love, and that comes from within. It's noble and all... to figure this out and make the statement that you're going to focus on self-love, but where do you even start? There is value in knowing yourself in many aspects of life outside of your love life, but how do you get there?

I want to be clear with my messaging; starting the journey of self-love doesn't need to happen when you're single or when you're feeling down on yourself. It just takes you to commit to this journey, hitting the key targets and being as real with yourself as possible. The first step I took was setting the right boundaries between myself and my partner. The second step was taking time to identify my wants and needs in order discover the real me. The third step is getting to a place of peace and knowing that at the core, I am okay alone. Those series of targets have helped me find true love in myself and my current partner. I eventually titled these series of targets as a self-love journey starting with dating myself.

Before we dive into the dating component of this segment, I think it's important to focus on loving yourself first. An exercise I recommend is to jot down different ways to love yourself. Think through real-life examples, as we all love in different ways and across various spectrums. A good starting point is to unpack moments where we felt special. For instance, a person may make you feel special by remembering your birthday or asking you to a dance. We all like to feel that people think about us and that we're thought about in a different way from others. You may like that someone notices you play with your hair when you get nervous or that your eyes turn green in a certain light. In a fast world of technology and instant gratification, who really knows you? Who sits down with you and is present in that moment?

While writing this segment, I was curious about what made other people feel loved and cared for. I met a woman in a lounge of an airport and asked her what specifically makes her feel loved. I asked what attributes she values. She paused, blushed a little and smiled as she replied, "You know, at first I thought it was about the gifts and affection, but as I get older, it's someone that sits with you, I mean really sits with you in the good moments and bad. That's what matters."

I found myself agreeing wholeheartedly. We underestimate moments of being present. Simply being there can be 95% of what we need from others. Sometimes, someone just holding your hand and being there in silence feels as powerful and life-changing as our favorite rallying cries. That element of presence felt like a great target within this journey of dating yourself. Sit and be present with yourself. Sometimes it may be accompanied by music, but maybe you just need to sit in silence and hold your own hand.

Establishing boundaries with yourself or with a partner (if applicable) is critical to this process. If you can commit to dating yourself one day month, make sure you are intentional about this time. Being intentional may mean scheduling appointments in advance, turning your phone off, or socializing with friends and family on this self-care day. Treat it just as if you are going on a first date. Give your girlfriends the heads up, a plan is made, and during the time of your date they are your sole focus. Once you've scheduled the time on the calendar, it's time to think about what you truly enjoy doing.

The first time I approached this step, I felt that I don't really enjoy being alone. I wondered how I could even imagine scheduling time with myself if I don't enjoy it! From my experience, I can promise you that this feeling will evolve with time. My first scheduled time was getting a glass of wine after work alone. It sounds dramatic, but after years of having a solid girl group and a long-term relationship, the thought of sitting alone at a bar made me feel sick. I forced myself to do this repeatedly. I modeled this after my stretch challenges at work. In order to sharpen your skills and overcome weaknesses, I've always been determined to take on professional challenges, from planning better team meetings to overcoming my fear of public speaking. Early in my career, public speaking also made me feel sick - and it still makes me feel uneasy - but

I was committed to getting over that fear and removing these weak parts of me. That was the a-ha moment; it's not that I didn't enjoy being alone. I was just afraid of change. Nailed it! Now that I know it's the anxiety of possibly always being alone, I could work on that aspect. This gift of self-awareness only came from being intentional about this time with myself and being honest with myself in order to progress. So focus on being present with yourself, schedule the needed time, and begin the self-assessment. Through feeling all the emotions that arise in this process, we are also healing and becoming more self-aware, which will only benefit us in the long run. These are the exact steps we take when meeting someone new that we're interested in. Be present with this person, be consistent with scheduling follow-up dates, and begin to assess whether this is someone you enjoy.

The self-assessment piece will eventually get you to the second target: identifying the true you. When we go on dates, we tend to share the same basic stories: I grew up in Connecticut, went to college, worked in banking, blah, blah. But what sets you apart from the crowd? Do you know that answer? Do you have the confidence to say what your worth is to a crowd of people or even to yourself? A part of loving someone is trying to understand them at their core, for better or for worse. Just setting the time will not get you to fall in love with yourself.

Another recommended exercise is to write down what makes you uniquely you. It can be physical or a personality trait, but make sure it's genuine and something you love about yourself. I know I'm a great listener. I know when I love someone, I'm all in, and that means I will dedicate all my time to get to know them inside and out. I pay special attention to those I care for and try to be kind to everyone I meet. I know that I have a smile that makes other people feel something. Those are the things I love about myself, and I hope it can inspire other people to pay attention to what makes them uniquely them.

We must understand what the attributes of love are and how to identify and act on them ourselves. Reflecting on how you love and how you like to be loved will be helpful in your exploration. At this stage in our lives, we recognize that love should hold no judgment. That is another recommendation I have: during this process, don't judge yourself for how you feel or when you feel. It's okay to have bad days where you don't feel in love with yourself. Maybe you've let someone down or haven't performed well at work, etc. The reality is that we're human and all deserve compassion, especially with ourselves. As I mention to my partner all the time, it's easy to be happy and to love when things are good. However, when we fight, I need us to be graceful with each other and remember that this too shall pass. That also applies to how we treat ourselves. Negative self-talk is toxic; we make mistakes, and we move on, period. To begin or reinforce our self-love, we should always be thinking about the types of love that we need to be well-rounded and happy.

My first experience with love started with my mother. This love grew through boundless affection, selflessness, protection, and unwavering support. My love for friends came from them stepping up and giving me confidence and support when they aren't obligated to, whereas parents may feel obligated. Friends choose to be in our lives because of the specific qualities we bring into the relationship. No matter who you love, that relationship needs to be nurtured. The fact of the matter is that love isn't unconditional, despite what the RomComs tell us. This is a factor we need to face as we begin the journey of self-love. Loving yourself needs to be consistent and will always need to be nurtured throughout time. A way to solve for this…date yourself.

I used to travel for work often and would typically order room service, listen to a podcast, maybe work out, and go to sleep. For some with kids at home, this may sound like a 5-star vacation, but for a woman with no kids, it was boring and lonely. This felt like a good opportunity to repurpose this time. I made a mind-set change that maybe going to grab a glass of wine isn't exciting enough for me to maintain this self-love journey. Like traditional dating, you want to make up activities that excite you. As mentioned previously, this practice of dating yourself should be sustainable.

I began to make a list: ok, I'll be in Philly for a three-day meeting. Have I seen those steps that were in that Rocky movie? Wait - have I even seen Rocky? Do I know what a Philly cheesesteak tastes like? Do I even know what the Liberty Bell looks like? I considered all of these things to be first date ideas.

So the plans are made, and now it's time to get dolled up! This is an important factor; I don't want to assume that all appreciate a glam squad, but getting ready for yourself is imperative! If sweats make you feel loveable, go with that. If it's getting their hair done and putting on that dress that's collecting dust in the closet, just do it! This area is really what excites me the most. I'm 5'9" and like to wear heels. This was a moment I could wear my tallest heels and not worry about towering over my date because - guess what - I am my own date!

Once the plans are made it's time to acknowledge any feelings that are bubbling up. The inner dialog was starting to get louder, "OMG! People must be wondering why I'm doing this alone!" "Will they wonder why I'm all dressed up!? Will they think I've been stood up?" "I'm pretty sure they think I'm late for drag brunch in my 6 inch platform heels and bright red lips."

All these ideas are totally self-centered. The reality of my internal dialog was that all my anxieties were grounded in feeling insecure about being alone. Typically, when you're all dressed up, your girlfriends are, too. Dating yourself means there is no longer a crutch to lean on. There was light at the end of the tunnel, however. The more I did things alone, the better I felt. Just like my public speaking stretch challenges, it will be painful in the beginning, but it will get better. That became my internal mantra: keep going, and it will get easier. To capture your thoughts and feelings, I recommend journaling your experiences. It may be helpful to look back and reflect on various moments on this journey. What felt bad? What felt good? What were you proud of? What made you uncomfortable? What made you feel brave? What dates do I like? Which don't I like? Being able to reflect will only help you to course correct and improve going forward. At the end of the day, this is a challenge, but it's meant to be enjoyable.

After two or three months, I began to reflect on the dates I went on with myself. I went to all the art exhibits I wanted to. When I did attend an event, I didn't feel rushed or pressured to leave within an hour. Due to my hypersensitivity to being alone, I was surprised at how many others attended events alone too. Surprisingly, I never went on a date with myself where I didn't speak to another person. I found myself meeting like-minded people who were happy to talk to a stranger. Even though I was on a date alone, sometimes I'd meet people or groups who invited me to join them, and I never said no. I tried to say yes to most things, and it helped me make friends and explore new places. These moments of what I considered bravery and open-mindedness were and still are invaluable. Because of these actions when I finally made the decision to get a divorce, I already knew I could do this alone. I could enjoy my life without a partner to lean on. More importantly, I started to believe that I was interesting, I did in fact have things to talk about, and the world is kind to you if you let it be. I knew at my core that I would be able to love again because I started to witness a new face in the mirror. This woman was interested in exploring herself through exploring different aspects in her life. She was no longer chasing fear but learning to love how independence feels. With this newfound awareness and mindset, I finally got to the third target: I'm fine alone.

Being fine alone doesn't mean we become so independent that we avoid relationships. On the contrary, the more you love yourself, the more you love and attract others. When you take time to learn about yourself, you're building self-esteem, which helps to expand your capacity for overall happiness. When you take the time to reflect on your own journey, you'll typically be more compassionate to others because you remember that we've all faced trials and tribulations. I think about the most vulnerable points in my own journey, and those were my strongest moments. Being fine alone is not even the true feeling. When you are happy with yourself and focused on continuous improvement, there is no time to feel alone. You will feel fulfilled, active, and motivated. Finding self-love is becoming full.

The biggest benefit of dating yourself and taking this journey to self-love is that you're working toward collecting qualities no one can take from you. Self- love cannot be taken from you, which is why I stress this practice whether you're single or in a relationship. There have been times that I feel lonely single, but not as lonely as I have felt in some relationships. It's most important to stay true to yourself while maintaining a relationship. I often have to remind myself that these are the qualities my partner likes, and it lets me remember to be myself – to be goofy, to always enjoy a laugh. However, I can only be my most beautiful if I also feel it.

How will you love another if you don't love yourself? That's another cliché I was sick of hearing, but that's because I had no idea how to start. It just takes you to commit to this journey, hitting the key targets and taking some of my recommendations to jot down moments to reflect on. If you are as real as possible with yourself, that drives you toward persistent growth and improvement. Once those intentions are set, you can pivot toward the key targets. It begins with setting the right boundaries between yourself and your partner, ensuring that you take the time to identify your wants and needs to discover the real you. Lastly, if you follow the path, you'll find yourself in a state of peace and knowing: a knowing that you are, in fact, fulfilled and fine being alone. Those series of targets have helped me find true love in myself and an ability to love others. I give all the credit to this concept of dating myself.

I wish I could say that I invented this concept, but I didn't. I believe I approached this self-love journey in a unique way and made it my own, which I charge you with. This is not only for people looking to begin to love themselves but also for people who want to continue to love themselves. By establishing boundaries, identifying the true you, and finding peace with being alone, you create the path toward sustainable self- love.

Chapter 8

A Ready Heart

by Chaun Pinkston

One of my greatest delights is spending heart-to-heart time with women. I love being a woman and being around other women drawn together in likenesses, differences, shared histories, and a plethora of issues that one can understand only by being a woman. In our time together, we discover how our lives are not so different, although the surface may appear so. But when we go deeper-beneath the outward appearances- we come to see that we all have the same core need. We need to connect to something greater than ourselves, something significant that compels us to want to become better versions of ourselves. Although there are many titles we may answer to - such as woman, wife, mother, sister, auntie, friend, cousin, daughter, neighbor, and boss - there is only one title that concretely grounds every part of our being, situating us in the center of a continuous and perfecting strength. We are called Beloved. And our Great and Loving God looks past our flesh, faults, and daily makeup disguises and calls us His.

You are called to live a life filled with purpose and passion. I want to encourage you to pursue that life, to put away the doubts, the fears, the personal judgments, and those lying voices that tell you that you are not good enough, not qualified enough, either too young or too old; they are lying voices meant to lure you away from fulfilling God's purposes in your life. And yes, there are multiple purposes. Too many people think there is just one particular thing we are meant to do with our whole lives. I assure you that God had more than one reason to redeem your life from sin and death. There is so much more to your life. There are people whose lives are and will be made better because of you.

"For we are His workmanship [His own master work, a work of art] created in Christ Jesus [reborn from above-spiritually transformed, renewed, ready to be used] for good works, which God prepared [for us] beforehand [taking paths which He set], so that we would walk in them [living the good life which He prearranged and made ready for us]. Ephesians 2: 10 amp.

If God created paths for you to walk in, He has purposes for you to fulfill. I pondered what I could share in twelve pages that would compel you to live with more inspiration and hope as you walk the paths God has already prepared for you. I recognize from my life that it is difficult to see your own light, but it is there, doing what light does – illuminating the darkness and being light. Hoping that you would never have a dark day would be naive of me, because dark days will come for all of us without notice and sometimes with no apparent cause. But, I can hope that the light in you will speak beyond the darkness, reminding you that it is there, ready to be light. God has created the paths you will walk. He knows every detour, every pit stop, and every wrong decision that leads to an abrupt lane change or what appears to be a dead-end. He also knows how to get you back on the right path at the right time because you are Called.

"You, Lord, keep my lamp burning; my God turns my darkness into light." Psalms 18:28.

As a wife of twenty-eight years, mother of two grown children and one child still in grade school, a grandmother (although I look way too young), a business owner with fifteen employees, and an anointing for preaching, I have plenty of testimonies and stories to share about walking paths that lead to dead ends but eventually working out for my good. There is also much I could share about how my light inspires others to find theirs, but my goal for these pages is to encourage you not by my story alone but by helping you see the power in yours and to know that there is still much more to your story.

I have a question to ask you to consider. The answer can determine how you see your story and whether your story is filled with faith and joy or with doubt and shame. The question is: How is your heart? To accept that you are called to a higher way of living in God is also to believe that you are a unique and special being made up of a spirit, a soul, and a body. Although you are a three-part being, there is one significant thing that each part of you shares interdependently: your heart.

Many of us have heard our grandmothers say, "Lord, Bless their hearts," often using the phrase when someone has done something they would call foolish. I know I gave the adults in my family plenty of opportunities to say, "Lord, Bless her heart." Now that I'm an adult, I understand this phrase so much more that I think we should change the way we greet one another from "How are you doing?" to "How is your heart?" To answer the question truthfully, the person answering has to be willing to be vulnerable. We all know how difficult it is to put yourself out there, especially when you don't know the intentions and motives of the other person. Also, the person asking has to be sincere. Asking someone how your heart is requires real connection and engagement. The question mandates a shift in how we relate to one another. It requires honest and authentic relationships, relationships that protect rather than manipulate, and relationships built with the anatomy of care. So, how's your heart? That's a real question I want you to hold for a moment.

The heart is a small organ that only weighs about a pound, but the condition of the heart affects our everyday lives spiritually, mentally, and physically; therefore, it is essential for you to have a strong, clean, willing, and believing heart. What do I mean by a Ready Heart?

Well, to be ready for something means to be in a suitable state for an activity, action, or situation, and to be fully prepared. One of my favorite examples of a ready heart is from the movie The Passion of the Christ.

Jesus, played by Jim Caviezel, was captured by Roman soldiers. He was stripped of his clothes, chained, and bound. The crown of thorns was stabbed onto his head so blood ran down his face. He was about to be beaten with the cat o' nine tails. The camera shot moves from a long shot showing his entire body to a close-up of his face. His lips move just enough to utter in Aramaic, "My heart is ready."

There, amid turmoil, Jesus, now bound, bloody, and bruised, prepares his heart for what he is about to experience. Like Jesus, we must also prepare our hearts for what we are about to experience. Sometimes, we must prepare our hearts for the pain, pressure, and uncertainty well before peace comes. If you take a moment to think about your life, you will see from your story that you have had moments of pain, pressure, and uncertainty, but you made it through. You did overcome. You have a story to tell about your triumph. I don't know if you took an inventory of your heart during those hard times. You may have felt that you didn't have peace, or you felt angry and anxious and didn't know what to do. Somehow, you made it to the other side. Thank God! But as you continue to journey in faith with God, I hope that you will become more aware of the condition of your heart every day because it is significant to the life you live, and the life you live reflects the condition of your heart.

Proverbs 4:23 in the New Living Translation says, *"Guard your heart above all else, for it determines the course of your life."*

You cannot guard what you do not regard. You must take care of your heart by taking inventory of what it carries. What emotions are spewing from your heart? What about the emotions that are unsurfaced? Even those matter in the course of your life. Yes, you may experience anxiety, which is very real and affects so many people. How you deal with anxiety may be different than how I deal with it, but what is common between us is that our hearts feel the weight of anxiety, and our heart knows the issues we face. But this is not dreaded news! We can do something about what our heart holds and its condition. We can engage the matters of our heart without fear, in our own time and unique way, by just beginning to recognize that the condition of our heart matters. By first recognizing your heart's condition, you can then slowly begin taking more control of what is stored in your heart and be more in control of how you allow it to affect your life.

To help you begin taking steps toward becoming more aware of the condition of your heart, I have a huge ask. Write down a few circumstances or situations in your life right now that you would describe as challenging or painful, something that you would like to be on the other side of. Describe each circumstance and be truthful with yourself. I will not ask you to share this with anyone unless you choose to. After describing the situation as you see it, write how you feel about each situation. Be honest with yourself. Is your heart feeling insecure, angry, ashamed, or betrayed? Try to gauge how your heart feels about each situation because the condition of your heart matters. Whatever you are experiencing, walking through, enduring, and even neglecting to deal with, the condition of your heart matters. I can't say it enough. The condition of your heart is significant to the life you live, and the life you live reflects the condition of your heart.

Here are some facts about the heart that may help you to understand why the heart matters so much and deserves daily attention. The heart is an organ and is considered the ruling center of the entire body. It is part of the body's circulatory system, transferring nutrients to cells, tissues, and all parts of the body. Other organs in the human body can fail and a person can still live with help from medical devices, medication, operations, etc., but when the heart stops beating, life ends. The heart is in control.

"As Water Reflects the face, so one's life reflects the heart." Proverbs 27:19,

Heart disease can be detected, but heart dis-ease can't be until your life reflects it. The heart matters, and the condition of your heart has consequences and directly affects how your story is shaped. I shared with you that it's not my intention to tell you so much about my life, but rather to remind you of the power that lies within your own life, but I do want to briefly share something from my life that has shaped me into the woman I am today.

There was a time when I hated being a wife. I regretted standing in front of over 150 people confessing my eternal love for a man who had become someone I hated living with. Asking my husband if he has to breathe is a sign of serious problems in our marriage. Just hearing his breath made my flesh crawl. Saying that I was unhappy is an understatement. I was a mad black woman out for blood. Looking in from the outside, we had obtained the American dream. We had a beautiful home, two children, good incomes, and sat on the front row at church. We were accomplished, but we were miserable and living with problems that could not be detected by the outside world. Adultery, lies, mistrust, lack of respect, resentment, fear, anger, unforgiveness, and a host of other negative influences, emotions, and behaviors framed our inner world.

Desperately wanting to stop the pain, but having no one to run to for help, the only way to escape was divorce. I wanted out, and nothing was going to stop me - not even God - because after all, I was the injured party, so God was on my side, right? It was simple to me. Go to the court, file for divorce, sign the papers, and I would be done! The bleeding stops, my heart no longer feels the pain of betrayal, my smiles become genuine with a newfound freedom that comes after a successful escape. Whew! Here comes happiness.

Well, it wasn't that simple. Despite being set on divorcing my husband (and he seemed to be fine with it), one day he blurted out, "I want my family!"

I laughed until I almost peed my pants, then I got angry and looked for something to throw at him while I yelled, "You don't want a family, you just want the security a family gives you. You want the illusion of a family without doing the work that is required to sustain one!"

It was in that last statement that God challenged me with the very accusatory words I spit out to my husband. Feeling angry and accused, I stormed out the room, not knowing what God wanted from me.

Now, if you are a wife and happen to feel this way, please do not take my brief synopsis and try to make it fit your situation. Every marriage is different and requires the path that God has set before it. For me, it was a long path of obedience to God. It wasn't easy or quick but took years. Now, celebrating 28 years, I can honestly say from my heart that I love my husband. I am so thankful to God that I did the hard work, the stuff that I didn't want to do. When I finally stopped kicking and screaming against what God was leading me to do, a breakthrough came. Again, it was a long road. My heart had to be ready to let go of things. My heart felt comforted by some of the negative feelings it was holding, and I actually felt justified by the anger and the resentment. I believed I had a right to it. Trust me that when I believe that I have a right to something, it takes God and all the angels to prove me wrong. Thankfully, God was up to the fight, because I was not giving in easily.

Again, my disclaimer is that you have to make your own decisions, and you have to decide what is best for you in every situation. For me, the path was reconciliation with my husband. It was costly and painful, and I regretted being on that path many times over, but I stayed on it and eventually landed in a sweet place. My heart eventually let go of the things it needed to as I learned to engage with my heart in truth. I gave the matters of my heart time to process their way through and, of course, I gave God room to speak to my heart, helping me whenever I got stuck. I hear wives spitting out the phrase, "It takes two to make a marriage work." And, yes, amen, it does, but it begins with one. As I shared, it was a long, difficult path to walk. But now, on the other side, it was worth it. My husband would tell you that I was the one to begin to walk toward healing and restoration in our marriage. I was the chosen one! And God was the one to finish it. My husband did make the necessary changes to support our path toward healing. He had to, or we would not be here today as a married couple. He had to acknowledge his own struggles and issues for restoration to come. He and I both had to work hard. So, there is no such thing as a wife changing her husband, making him become a better man who makes better decisions. Ultimately, he will have to want to change and be willing to work alongside you to make things better.

Having the opportunity to minister to wives is a privilege that I honor, and I will never take it for granted. I do not push my testimony on other wives because my testimony is unique to my family and me.

A READY HEART

What I do urge a wife to do is to consider the condition of her heart because a disobedient heart has consequences, an unbelieving heart has consequences, an unwilling heart has consequences, a manipulating heart has consequences, a fearful heart also has consequences, as does as a faithful heart. Evaluating the condition of your heart is always a good place to start when you pursue any kind of change. It is an honest place.

The condition of your heart is significant to the life you live, and the life you live reflects the condition of your heart. So, I ask again, how is your heart? How is the ruling center of the whole person leading you?

I want to spend the last part of our time together examining one area that leads to more understanding about what we can do to guard our hearts.

I shared earlier that a Ready Heart is a heart that is in a suitable state for an activity, action, situation, trial, challenge, or opportunity, and when the heart is operating properly, its chambers are providing vital oxygen, nutrients, and purities that we need throughout the body. But just as there are physical purities and nutrients that the heart funnels through the body, tangible properties that can be seen or measured like blood or how much oxygen the body receives, there are also impurities and intangible properties that the heart has to manage. There is one area of intangibles that the heart has to manage that can't be seen with the naked eye or measured with some type of medical device. It can be either harmful or helpful to the heart and to the body. Although this area of intangible matter can't be measured, what it produces certainly materializes in every area of our lives. Do you have any idea what this intangible matter is that our heart has to manage? The intangible matter is our thoughts.

"For the weapons of our warfare are not carnal but mighty in God for pulling down strongholds, 5 casting down arguments and every high thing that exalts itself against the knowledge of God, bringing every thought into captivity to the obedience

of Christ." 2 Corinthians 10:4-5.

Our thoughts can be pure or impure, and blockages are the result of impurities that the heart cannot funnel through. Our thoughts can provide a healthy channel of nutrition or be a funnel for harmful bacteria. Basically, our thoughts are either life-giving or destructive to our whole being.

I read an illustration a while ago that talked about the mind-heart connection or the attitude of the mind. This is a way of thinking of a person or situation which directly results in a spiritual or physical manifestation of that way of thinking. For instance, if you wake up and the first thought is that it will not be a good day, you will likely experience a rough day. I have learned to recognize that when I get tired in my mind so follows my words, feelings, and actions, and now what flows through my heart is evident in my life. I get irritable and easily agitated. Understanding the need to guard your heart does not mean it is easy to do. I have gotten better at discerning the condition of my heart more quickly when I feel anxious or fearful or angry, and my response time has improved, but guarding the heart is an active process that you must be intentional about engaging in.

I love the biblical story about the Shunammite Woman. It takes place in 2 Kings 4: 8-37. The prophet Elisha goes into the town of Shunem where a woman of prominence, the Bible points out, invites him to stay with her and her husband. She gives him his own room with a bed, a chair, and a lamp and tells him that any time he is in town, he is welcome to stay with them. He receives her kindness, and before leaving, Elisha asks the woman if he can do anything for her. She graciously declines, but Elisha's servant, Gehazi, tells Elisha that she is without a child, and Elisha declares to her that she will have a child this time next year. The Shunammite woman responds peculiarly, "No, my lord. O man of God, do not lie to your maidservant."

She conceived and had a son. Later in the story, the son becomes ill and dies in his mother's lap. I don't know about you, but I would have had some choice words for the man of God and for the God he served because the son I didn't even ask for died. But the Shunammite woman gives us a glimpse of a Ready Heart in action. She takes her son's lifeless body to the room she had prepared for Elisha, laying him on the bed and shutting the door behind her. She tells her husband to send one of the servants and a donkey to take her to the man of God. Her husband asked what the reason was, but her reply was simply, "It will be alright." She tells the servant to move fast. Elisha sees the woman approaching and sends Gehazi to ask her if all is well with her and her family. Without hesitation the Shunamite woman replies, "All is well." But Elisha perceives that she is distressed, and she tells him that her son is dead and insists that he goes back with her. The story ends with Elisha raising her son from the dead. This was a miracle, but the point of the story is that amid her pain and turmoil, her world being shaken by the death of her son, and undoubtedly with a heart distressed and burdened, the Shunamite woman did speak from the place she was, she spoke from the place of where she was going. She told her husband it would be alright, and she told the man of God all was well. I know her thoughts were rambling, and questioning; maybe she couldn't think at all, but her response shaped her story. Death didn't take her son that day.

What is shaping your story? Let it be words of faith. Thoughts that stimulate a healthy, clean, and strong heart. What are the issues in your life? Let me remind you that the condition of your heart reflects the condition of your life. Do the heart work so that you can walk ready to face every season of your life. Remember the story I shared earlier about the character of Jesus in The Passion of the Christ. He declared that his heart was ready before the first slash against his body. Likewise, the Shunammite woman declared that all was well even before she reached the man of God. The paths that led each of them to their situations were different, but what is similar in each of their stories is the condition of their hearts. They spoke to their situation and not from it. Their story didn't end the way it looked like it would. Victory did come to both Jesus and the Shunammite woman, despite their circumstances, just as victory will come to you. And just like their stories are still being told, so will yours because there is so much more to your story, and I declare by faith that your *Heart is Ready*.

Chapter 9

Flight or Fight: A Redemptive Story

by Jae Hunter

WHO'S SLEEPING WITH YOUR HUSBAND TOO?

A few years ago, I thought I had it all. I had just married the man that I thought I had prayed for all my life. I had a beautiful wedding, a celebrity style event. I had DJ Spinderella and Monie Love MC at my wedding. Our businesses were growing and thriving. My husband and I had just grossed our first million dollars in business. We had managed to build the house of our dreams and purchased every status-symbol car imaginable. I thought to myself, Girl, you made it!! You've arrived!

You see, I come from a middle income home, set with good morals and values and with education and faith being the foundation of my upbringing. But, in my early adulthood I went rogue for many years. After leaving an abusive marriage, I ended up homeless with four kids in tow. That's another story and chapter all on its own. But, imagine being at your lowest point in life − or so you think - and fighting hard to climb back up. It's no easy feat, but with the foundation of my faith and grit, I came out ahead. When I finally remarried and had reached ultimate status, I was on cloud 9, but…

My beautiful little bubble would soon burst. Shortly after my wedding, I found out my husband had been cheating on me, and this destroyed me. I didn't have physical proof, but I found multiple conversations on his phone that he had with multiple women, and as the saying goes, if it walks like a duck and talks like a duck, honey…it's a darn duck!

Not the man that I thought was the last good man on this planet! Not the man that I had heavily prayed for and believed the good Lord had sent to me. How could he do this to me? To me!!! A beautiful woman - who helped him build his dream! To me - the woman who took in his kids! To me! The woman who was tending to his beautiful surroundings, the woman who did everything for everyone!

I'm not the kind of woman who gets cheated on! So, how in hell did this happen to ME! But you know the saying: be careful what you pray for. Later, I would find out exactly how prayer works and how God's sense of humor can be a little twisted at times - or at least it may seem like it. In the end, it's a hard lesson that you were destined to learn, not just so that you can be delivered from it, but so that your story can then be a testament to others and that your purpose can be found. Let me tell you ladies, when you pray for that spouse, be specific down to the miniscule details. When I prayed, I thought I was being specific. My husband checked off most of my prayer list, but I failed to include loyalty.

You would think that I would leave after finding out about his indiscretions, right? I sure as heck wanted to! But no, I stayed. The reason was beyond me at the time. All my friends and family were rooting for me to end my marriage. I'm sure that all of my husband's family and friends were rooting for the same as well. You see, envy carries a heavy weight. Success carries a heavy weight, and Ego carries a heavy weight. My husband and I eventually figured out how all of these things were factors in our near demise.

This was the trifecta that spurred the beginning of a year of pure HELL! Baybay, when I tell you pure HELL, I don't think you can even imagine the hell that I lived through - that my entire family would live through during this year.

I was the angry scorned woman. *Diary of a Mad Black Woman* had nothing on this real life trailer. After I found out ALL that happened prior to and right up to my wedding, I was flabbergasted! All the questions arose in my head, like how, when?! We both worked from home, so how did he manage to get away and have the time to have not one, but multiple affairs - How did he sneak around and have access to talk to one of my girlfriends when I was always right next to him? How did I not see the interest that my girlfriend had in him? Every time I thought about it, it just angered me more. The betrayal and hurt caused the anger to set in,and the anger boiled so intensely that it literally caused me to become numb for a long, long time. You know the saying: once a woman goes silent, watch out!

But here's the plot twist: that entire year after the affair, when I'd go to church or just when I was in the presence of the Lord, the message for me that year was, "Be Still." And I don't mean I had just read a passage once and saw that phrase and thought, "Oh He's telling me to be still." No, the Lord was placing that message everywhere, Like Billboard status. If I opened up myBible, it was there. If I read a book, it was there. One day, I was in the church bookstore trying to find books for my daughters. A bracelet kept calling me. When I looked at it in tiny print, it had the words "BE STILL" engraved on it. I thought, "Okay, Lord, I hear ya, I'm gonna sit my big behind right here and I'm going to obey and Be Still."

But here's the thing, ladies: I was sitting still in my own way, NOT in the Lord's way. I had a lot of learning still to do! I was still stuck in a place of anger and feeling so betrayed that I was continuously operating from a point of flesh instead of faith.

I sat still and stayed in my marriage, though no one understood why. All of my friends thought I was stupid for first allowing such behavior, but also the betrayal that was the cause of the very toxic behavior we put each other through that year. When I say toxic, I mean like if Iyanla was in my house watching us, she would've whooped both of us into shape and even made a grown man cry.

We yelled, screamed, and constantly used profanities in front of the kids, just completely disrespecting each other and our household. Many nights, I got so angry that I threw things at him. All I felt was anger, and I wanted him to hurt.

One day in particular, my cleaning ladies were over, and I had just hired an attorney to weigh options for my impending divorce. My attorney had advised me to be sure to secure my finances. He had seen many business partnerships destroyed through divorce, so I was minding P's and Q's, making sure every I was dotted and every T crossed! My husband is a smart, calculating man, but I thought I was smarter and more than capable of making sure I kept what was rightfully mine so I could walk away with what was rightfully due to me. After all, I had helped him build this entire mini empire. I had to think like a man in order to win this case. That song by Mary J kept playing in my head, "No, I'm not gonna cry, oh, I'm not gonna cry, I'm not gonna shed no tears." You know the one...

That morning, I went to the bank to take my half of the balance out, and when I tell you I literally missed the clock by a few minutes, I am not exaggerating. This man had just left our bank 5 minutes before me. Mind you, I tried to be at the bank right when it opened, but as luck would have it, I was a few minutes late. He beat me to the punch and emptied out our bank account. He created an entirely new account that I had no access to.

At that moment, I thought, "Okay you want to play dirty. Then so can I." I froze our business account, took him off as a signer, and tried to make sure that no more funds were moved until we figured out our next move. Needless to say, I was beyond livid. I came home in a straight rage! I walked in the house screaming, yelling, and cursing. I grabbed everything I could get my hands on and threw a sheer fit. I broke a few things, and my poor cleaning ladies were probably thinking that this little Latina lost her mind! Not to mention, I had just destroyed their good work! I remember my husband calmly asking what I was doing, acting like nothing had just happened.

That made me even more furious. The audacity of him to ask why I was so upset! I was just plain nasty and screamed back," I don't give a flying f. That's their darn job, and they can clean the mess up. Maybe you can go cheat with one of them now, too!

I'm telling you the exact verbiage to show you that pain causes us to come out of our character. Being ugly like that to a set of women who had never done anything to me except take care of my house was not who I was or even am. I'm a very caring and nurturing person. I am the type of woman who will give the shirt off her back and her last dollar away to complete strangers. I'm the type of woman who swerves for a squirrel in the road because I don't want to run it over. I hate hurting people, I hate confrontation, and I hate discord, but in this season of my life, Hurt would become my middle name. Just call me Miss Inflicting pain, because that's exactly what I did every chance I had.

But, you see, pain and anger are poison for your soul. It tears your soul down and makes you act in ways you'd never see yourself act. There were days that I fully understood the women on the show Snapped, because honey when I tell you I probably could've ended up in jail a time or two due to my rage during this season, I'm not playing. Ya girl should've been shackled and locked up or maybe even sent to a psychiatric hospital.

There would be dozens of these moments over the course of the year.

One day, after meeting our friends for a nice dinner, we started arguing in the car. Honestly, I couldn't even tell you today what that argument was about. I just remember him yelling at me, and I remember feeling confined and angry - and I don't mean just angry; I mean I saw red angry. I was possessed with anger, and I think I even remember seeing it in his eyes. He knew I was out of my mind with rage. We were stopped at a light, and I yelled for him to let me out of the car so I could walk home.

From the stop light to my house was about 2 miles. I thought to myself that I can make the trek, no biggie. Well, the light turned green. He was about to turn right, but in that instant, I jumped out of the car. It wasn't a stop-drop- roll kinda jump; it was just let me get the hell out, kinda jump. Even with the car barely moving, I was trying to be dramatic.In my rage, I jumped out and landed incorrectly. I hit the pavement hard enough that my ankle ended up under me.

At that moment, I thought that I probably just sprained my ankle, and the pain would subside. My adrenaline was at an all-time high, so I couldn't feel the pain. Now - don't get me wrong, my husband did try to talk some sense into me and get me back in the car, but my rage wouldn't let me see past that instance. He got tired of begging me and proceeded home.

I hadn't even walked a quarter of a mile when my foot just gave out. I couldn't walk at all. That is when the reality of what I had just done sank in: I could've killed myself. Now, here I was unable to walk, looking insane on the side of the road. I had to call my daughters and ask them to come get me. Imagine a mother having to call her daughters to rescue her. How in the heck was I going to explain this one? I couldn't. When I finally came to my senses, I was embarrassed and hurt, emotionally and physically. I ended up having to go to the orthopedic doctor and found out that my leg was fractured. I was in a cast for the next 6 weeks. All because I allowed my rage to take over.

Are you starting to see a pattern here? It was a year of pure self-destruction. And this was just the beginning.

Literally every other day was a fight. Many nights I slept away from my husband, leaving to go get a room at a nearby hotel. I was at my wits end. I was going out with my friends, the same friends who probably wanted to see us fail, probably the same friends who were after my husband, not because they wanted him, but because they wanted the lifestyle. But I didn't care, Jae was doing Jae!

The day of my daughter's 16th birthday, I had planned a beautiful outing. I rented a house in uptown Dallas, and had planned a nice dinner and evening out for her and a group of her friends. My sister and my close friend at the time joined us as well. After the girls were all settled in after dinner, my daughter said, "Mom, why don't you and your friends go out for a bit?"

I asked if she was sure, and she was. Of course, a group of 15-16 year olds just wanted full access to the house without hovering parents, so us moms decided to have a couple of drinks. Luckily for us, there was a little bar and grill right up the road, so we walked on over, sat at the bar, and ordered margaritas. All was right with the world for a moment, until...

Now, before I tell you what ensued next, let me just say: when people say Satan is on the prowl and he comes to only seek and destroy, that devil ain't no lie. In all the places, at all the given times, why on this particular night did an ex-boyfriend of mine walk into that bar? I'm not talking about an ex from like months ago or shortly before I met my husband. I'm talking about an ex who originally lived hundreds of miles away from where I now live. He immediately recognized me, took a seat, and started talking. I introduced him to my friend, and we allowed him to buy us a few drinks. The crazy part of it all is that this was an ex-boyfriend from about 20 years ago and he didn't even live in Dallas when I knew him, yet somehow here we both were. At the end of the night, without thought, I invited him back to the rental house. I know - right now you're literally gasping as you read this and you're saying, " Gurl!!! No, the heck you didn't!"

Let me tell you, yes, I sure did! This could've been a clip in a drama-filled movie. In my mind, I justified my actions because my husband had done it too. This is my ex, at least I knew him, he wasn't just some random guy. It felt good to go down memory lane. I felt nostalgic. I was getting closure to a long-lost chapter in my life. I felt wanted, I felt sexy, and above all else, I wanted revenge. I wanted to feel like I had won this battle.

But here's the thing: no one wins when your actions have the power to inflict so much hurt and pain. I was so involved in the "moment" that I totally disregarded my own child's milestone birthday. I was extremely selfish and didn't think about how she would feel. I did what I did in front of her friends, which made it even worse. That night,I was so oblivious and caught up in my own moment that I didn't realize my daughter knew. I brought someone in that night. In my head, I didn't think anyone would know; it was a 3-story house and he'd be gone by the morning.

Boy, was I wrong! In my daughter's embarrassment, she sent all her friends home that night. Imagine the horror when I found out she had to call all her friends' moms to come pick them up. I still cringe when I think about my actions that day. My daughter had also called my husband to pick her up.

When I woke up from my one-night rendezvous and was finally sober, all I heard was my husband banging on the door. I was terrified, and yet a part of me wanted him to catch me, which he did. He caught me in my birthday suit, lying next to another man! An argument ensued between my husband and the ex, and all I could do was lay there frozen and speechless.

When my husband finally came to me, obviously heart-broken and out of breath because I'm sure he was ready to kill a man, all I could muster the courage to say was, "It's Over!"

I told him to leave and to leave me alone. I told him I would come home later that day to pack up my things and move out. I was finally done!

When I finally arrived home later that evening, I couldn't even look at my family. The guilt was such a heavy weight to carry. All 9 of our kids knew that Mommy had stepped out on her marriage. I was so numb, nervous, and embarrassed. I had no explanation for my children. I was crying inside, yet I still had to put up the front of being strong and making it seem like it was my husband's fault for starting this entire nightmare first.

We lost a few good friends after my indiscretion. I'm sure my husband and I were a nightmare to be around, so many of our friends just didn't want to be around the drama. Half of my kids were team Mom, and the others were team Dad. It was a house divided, and each time any of us stepped into the room, you could cut the air with the pain and anger everyone was feeling.

That night, however, I didn't leave. I moved myself into our spare bedroom and tried to figure out what I really wanted. Seeing the kids so torn and confused hit me to my core. Having a blended family isn't easy. My kids had been raised by my husband and vice versa. We weren't just the usual step-dad and step-mom with no liabilities to divide, we were Mom and Dad. We had been raising these children together for years at this point, and it wasn't easy to just leave and be done.

My husband came into the room one night and just broke down. He looked so helpless and defeated. In the same breath that he said he hated me for my actions, he professed his love and claimed he didn't want to lose his marriage, his wife, or his family. Again, I deflected and pushed blame back on him, I broke down sobbing. I had one foot out the door, NO, actually I had 75% of my body out the door and one toe left on the ground across the threshold. But again, that little voice inside of me said,, "Be Still, "and so I did.

The days after that incident turned into weeks, and the weeks into months. Throughout those months, we went to counseling and to church. We talked to the friends we had left, who reminded us that marriage is hard; it is a daily choice to love each other every day even when we aren't performing at our optimal level. You know that quote, "Just two imperfect people learning to love."

I stayed in my word and in my faith and, somehow, day by day, we started to mend. My husband and I laid everything out on the line. We went back to the very beginning of why and how we got there. We were so in love and in sync in the beginning. How did we allow this to happen to us? Everyone thought we were this great perfect family - the power couple who together achieved their dreams - who were raising 9 kids full-time with no help and whose children also seemed to be perfect.

FLIGHT OR FIGHT: A REDEMPTIVE STORY

My husband and I started learning how to communicate effectively. If we were both going to stay, we had to learn how to forgive first and foremost, and we had to learn how to love each other again - and not just in the romantic way, but in the Biblical way. I had to learn how to be a Proverbs 31 wife.

I remember crying to my husband, asking him why, why did he even do what he did? I told him how I used to hold him on this huge pedestal. I had given him all of me, something I had never done with any other man in my life. I was 100% vulnerable, and yet it felt like he had slapped me in the face. His actions caused immense hurt. At the time, I didn't know how to get rid of that feeling. His only reply was- He was selfish. He wasn't thinking about me or the kids. He was just interested in the attention from the other women. As we dug deeper into the why's, we learned the psychological reasoning. You know the saying: "Hurt people, hurt people."

We learned that when you don't heal from adolescent hurts, you project those feelings and carry them with you into your adult life. I'm not making excuses for our actions at all; what I am telling you is that all the information is factual.

Cheating is never about just sex. It goes way deeper than just the physical.

You see, my husband came from nothing. He was born in Louisiana and became a city boy when he went to live with an aunt because his own stepfather was extremely abusive to him and his brothers. He once told me stories of how his step-father beat them, and would take all the money in the household to go buy drugs. There were days he and his brothers would go without any food and they would go to bed hungry. He felt abandoned by his mother; he felt neglected by the one person who was supposed to love him and protect him, yet she chose to support a horrible man over her own sons. This became the catalyst of my husband's horrible track record in relationships. It was the reason he didn't trust women, and it created deep- rooted insecurities within him, demons he still battles to this day.

So fast forward to when my husband and I started being successful. He had never seen that kind of money. Our money came fast, too. With it, our image changed. I would constantly remind him that he was the COO of a company now, so he needed to look the part. Well, those words later haunted me. Because no woman wants a scrub. She wants that sugar daddy type of man who's going to take care of her, right? The kind who's going to tell her she's beautiful, the kind who promises to always have her back. Well, that was my husband. And - the Jezebels swooned after him.

Imagine being a man who came from nothing, making it in the world. A world where the odds had been so stacked up against you your entire life, from the first woman you met to the last you had been hurt. At the time, He felt like he had power. I don't know what it is about men with money, but those thirsty women out there smell that scent from miles away. They are ready to pounce like a lion at any chance of having the same lifestyle that they see you living, unaware of the sacrifices you yourself made as a woman alongside your husband to get there, TOGETHER! So, when these women come onto him, they set the trap. He was caught like a rat in a mouse trap. Because he had a trusting, loving wife at home, he found it easy to continue - until he couldn't continue anymore because I pulled a checkmate on him!

Mommy and Daddy issues are real. Sadly, most of us don't know how to heal from these childhood traumas. Thankfully for us, we were ready to put in the work.

When it was my turn to speak in our therapy session, we discussed my why's. I never admitted to being selfish. Instead I admitted to wanting retaliation. I justified my actions by his actions. I told the therapist that it was cause and effect. I felt like he deserved it, and he got what he deserved. She looked at me like I was crazy, which maybe temporary insanity better described what I had just put us all through. However, through our sessions I acknowledged that we were both selfish; we were both destructive. Neither of us thought about our marriage, our children, or anyone outside of our own personal Ego. We had to check our Ego and tell her to kick rocks.

It was a humbling experience to say the least. By this point, we had made it all the way to final orders in divorce court. Yes, during this entire time we were still moving forward with the divorce. Yet, somehow, even that day we just sat with our attorneys and told them that we couldn't agree on the terms, so we'd have to go back to the drawing board. Oblivious to the fact that this must've just been the Lord doing his thing.

It's funny how God does things. At the time, I was so wishy-washy with what I wanted, in my spare time, I was trying to come up with plan B. I applied for rental houses but would get declined. I never understood why either, because I had great credit and way more than enough money. But God knew why.

During this time, we still co-existed under the same roof. We started surrounding ourselves with only our couple friends who had viable marriages. They became our support system. I'm not saying married people can't have single friends, but what I will tell you is that when your marriage is already in a vulnerable state, those single friends are like a child playing with matches. You open up Pandora's box when you surround yourself with people who are not on the same path as you. It was these friends who shared stories of their own marital struggles, and this gave us the enlightenment and wisdom that we needed to finally see that what we wanted was not divorce, but healing.

We even had a neighbor couple who walked the neighborhood every night, and it had to be nothing but God. One day as they walked, they stopped my husband. Somewhere between hello and goodbye, they gave him advice and told him a story about their own survival after indiscretions in their marriage.

Everyone we knew who had survived infidelity told us the same thing. The key to getting past it is faith and forgiveness. We had to put in the work and make the choice daily to fight for our marriage.

It took that entire year to begin the healing process, and when I tell you we serve a merciful God, he was beyond merciful. At the end of our self-destructive year, the tear-down of our mini empire was like a domino effect. We had managed to destroy our credit, and due to COVID our businesses had taken a hit. We had to rebuild not only our relationship and the way we would navigate through it but we had to rebuild our finances too. It was a long road back to redemption, and we are still presently in the great fight.

Let me tell you that it hasn't been an easy road. There are days my husband and I still argue. There are days he lets the devil win, and he'll remind me of my past faults. Men take longer to deal with infidelity because for them, their ego is forever bruised. For me, I made the conscious decision to let it go. I couldn't keep driving myself insane wondering why. I had to let it go for myself. The pain and memory will forever be imprinted in my heart and etched into my memory bank. But, if I was going to make this work, I had to forgive wholeheartedly. I told myself if I serve a God who can forgive multiple sins, then surely I can forgive my husband and learn to move forward.

My husband has again become my best friend, and I honestly can't envision a day without him. We truly are that power couple that so many wanted to see fail, but we called the devil a liar and showed that sucka who's boss! The hardest part wasn't even forgiving each other and learning how to effectively fight for our marriage. The hardest part was seeking forgiveness from our children and together as a family, fighting and teaching each other what a faith-centered marriage truly means. Half of our children are in their 20-s with their own relationships, and we have taught them what they should and shouldn't accept in a relationship. Now, don't get me wrong; I'm not telling every woman to accept cheating. I don't condone it; however, what I am here to say is that there is a rainbow at the end of a hurricane season. It is possible to come out on the other side intact after infidelity.

I rose like the phoenix and came out stronger because of this season. The crazy part about Biblical messages is that, after we started making amends, the next message I would receive was to Surrender. Surrendering it all to him, the Most High, he alone has the power to deliver you from any storm. Trust me when I say I've lived through many seasons, and I can give you 40 years of examples of how God did that in my life. I am a walking testament to his grace and glory. This is all but one chapter in a lifelong book of deliverance, redemption, mercy and grace.

I hope that if you're ever in a position such as mine, you heavily weigh your options. Don't be so quick to throw in the towel. Do the work to dig deep and figure out the root of the problem. Then, figure out how to come up with steps to deliver you from the problem. Once you start taking those steps and truly submit and are open to healing, I promise that whether you choose to stay like I did and fight, or if you choose to leave, you will come out ahead.

There are always brighter days ahead. I had many years of darkness in my lifetime, but now I'm living a life of authenticity, a life where my family and I practice forgiveness daily. We communicate daily, we say I love you daily, we express gratitude daily - and not just for the blessings he bestowed but also for the trials that he gives us. I now live a life where I've learned the true meaning of unconditional, unbreakable love. It is a life I now am proud to say that I've built and have found purpose in. I pray that you too find your purpose and do the work to live life fully and unapologetically. While I'm apologetic for my actions, I'm not apologetic about the lessons learned while I was stuck in the dark. It has brought me one step closer to fulfilling my destiny, and one thing I will never stop doing is working on myself daily. The story hasn't ended; it's only half written. Be the best–selling author of your own life. There are many empty pages still left to write.

Chapter 10

Trilogy of Life

by Dr. Donna Newman

Life is an adventure - a milestone that involves consistent momentum. As I wondered what I would write about in this anthology, I think about the many unshakable faith experiences I have had in which God made a presence. Everyone's trajectory is different. We experience circumstances in our own way. Life is a Rubik's cube, isn't it? I have found myself trying to figure out the perfect situation or circumstance. Life isn't perfect; it can be risky, yet life can be a product of a resilient attitude.

As a woman, we are geared to bounce back, build on our personal lessons with broad shoulders, maneuver relationships through love and make a difference. This life trilogy creates a picture of some of my life experiences that have allowed me to grow. Experiences are dealt with in different ways, yet they strengthen our inner woman to live the fulfilled life we are destined to live. *We either own our stories or they own us.* – Brene Brown

Trilogy: Part 1
"Being a mother is learning about strengths you didn't know you had and dealing with fear you didn't know existed." - Linda Wooten

I remember being enraptured with the birth of my son. Towards the end of my trimester, I held a picture of a sonogram which displayed a white halo around his head. To date, 30 years later, I remain unsure why it appeared, and little did I know that it would be an emotional roller coaster. My son wanted to enter this world on Memorial Day, although July 8th was his due date! From the minute the membranes surrounding my baby ruptured, my scenario became messy. There was a ride in an ambulance to a different hospital from the one where I had planned to deliver, complete bed rest, and painful injections to control oncoming contractions and to build my son's lungs. This was a time full of kerfuffle and uncertainty.

I consider myself a walking story - one that I believe is a testament of how precious life is and could be snippets of someone's similar experience. After being on complete bed rest for two weeks, it was time for this little man to enter the world eight days in; but wait, things again would continue to be messy. My son was breeched. An emergency c-section needed to happen. I saw my pre-mature son for the first five seconds of his life. For health reasons, I needed attended to.

Three days had gone by without another glimpse of my child. I remember fading in and out and not being aware of my surroundings. Well, during those three days, I began to hemorrhage and clot. The doctor, as painful as it was, had to roll his fist above my fresh stitches to expel the liver size blood clots which had formed in my body. This experience remained unshakable. I was so scared and emotional. What did I do wrong? Three days went by, and I still only had a glimpse of my son when he was extracted by cesarean section.

God knew my son was determined, strong-willed, and had something to say! He fought in the Neonatal Intensive Care Unit (NICU) for several weeks. I am thankful I was spared, and the man upstairs was doing and continues to do a good work in me. As I previously stated, my son had something to say in this world. This little boy with the halo over his head had a purpose. Today, he is consistently engaged in the word. He is touching the souls of the youth through his ministry.

Do I regret this experience? Absolutely not. There is no secret sauce to how our cards will be distributed. My lane of effort, or should I say my path here, was jolting but inspirational. We can't always see it, but God can take your mess and build you a kingdom. He will move mountains in our weakest moments of trust.

Philippians 4:6-7
"Don't worry about anything, but in everything, through prayer and petition with thanksgiving present your requests to God. And, the peace of God, which surpasses all understanding, will guard your hearts and minds in Christ Jesus.

Trilogy: Part 2

I have learned we are not promised tomorrow. I believe in taking chances and living your best life. Of course, it comes within our means and capability, yet being a pioneer of adventure is aligned with opportunity; no matter what that might mean for you. For me, pursuing an education was an easy decision. I love to learn. I love to navigate through the experience of dreams and goals. I find I am in the best place to learn when I'm in a different environment or surroundings other than my own.

So, I decided to take a trip with a friend who was pursuing their education and paving their professional path, just as I was. But my educational expedition came with the unexpected. I was headed to Miami, FL to spend some time working on my dissertation. Yes, Miami, and I was focused. I was determined to get the creative juices flowing through tenacity and the support of my friend. You see, having someone in your corner is important for trust and emotional support.

As I arrived at the Fort Lauderdale airport and headed to baggage claim, another traveler from a different flight alerted several of us that an active shooter was just two claim lanes down. Upstairs, within my view, was a restaurant. I gathered my luggage and took the escalator up. I sat at the restaurant and ordered a drink. Within ten minutes of my drink being placed on the table, all of us in the restaurant heard gunshot-like sounds.

We took shelter under the restaurant tables. The chaos was tremendous. Those in the corridors raced to the nearest exit doors. A mother was lying in front of me, crying hysterically, because in that split moment when people disbursed to feel safe, she couldn't see her children and was asking for them. I heard a female from across the room say, "Your children are safe and with me." It was that scene that validates the strength and support we see in other women. It screams, "I got you!"

In the meantime, my cell phone was on the table next to my drink. We were told by the police not to move. Snipers had moved into the building as well, and we were looking up from under the table at firearms. I felt the need to call my mother. She needed to know my current situation. I took a risk and crawled to the table to retrieve my cell phone. Thank the Lord it was still there. I was able to reach my sister first, who in turned reached our mother. They were not aware of the news, that the airport was on lockdown, or that people were wounded by the active shooter.

Time passed - two hours, as a matter of fact, lying under a table. Remembering to trust God, I thought of Ephesians 6:10-11, Be strong in the Lord. I needed to remain strong in his authority to stand against the evil spirit. I am convinced that, as women, we are built to stand strong even in times of turmoil. Everything in the airport was shut down (i.e, restaurants and bathrooms). After two hours, we eventually were able to move approximately 200 feet to the hallway leading to the airline gate area. There were people consoling one another and looking to charge cell phones. Was it a sense of relief? Not really.

There was still the unknown, and the snipers were present at each turn. There were many passengers unable to retrieve their luggage. This was my current season in life. I was on a path I had chosen to take and determined to achieve my personal goal. We never know when our story will change or shift. However, I am a believer in making the most of my moment.

I, along with others, sat in the hallway for an hour. I received calls from family concerned about my safety. I was okay in that moment. I was the gatekeeper of my emotions. Once we moved to a sitting area toward the gates, there were still limited resources for us. However, food and use of facilities became available. Now it was a waiting game, but circumstances led by God. He is in this. He dedicates his time in any given instant. This brings me to Romans 8:28: *And we know that in all things God works for the good of those who love him, who have been called according to his purpose.*

I recall landing in the early afternoon. The lockdown continued until the outside light became dark. I admit my feelings of anxiety and being overwhelmed remained in process mode. But Jo Petty said it best, "You can't control the length of your life—but you can control its width and depth." Again, I am working to unpack it all. Could it have been that my adrenaline is hiding the fact that I really do not have it all together?

As the time continued to tick away, exactly at the eighth hour, we began to move to the lower level. Still being guarded by what I considered massive men with guns, I had to listen very carefully to instructions. I prayed to God to release any feelings of helplessness and assure me that things would be okay. I repeated to myself, "I am gonna make it. I have too much work to do! I am here for a purpose." Whether that meant to continue my education, listen to someone else's story, or reassess my internal being, I needed to give it to God.

My plan was to get to Miami. Sometimes we as women do what we have to do to get things done. Of course, in a good way. I did not have a vehicle, and those allowed to leave the airport had to have a vehicle there. The situation was still very chaotic. People were not listening to the police officers. They would not stay stationary as requested. There was an Uber driver who was stranded when the roads were shut down. It took a minute, but the driver was a lifesaver. I hopped in the SUV, and 30 minutes later made it to Miami!

I share this part of my life because it's okay to not be okay in moments of uncertainty. Quite frankly, it took several months to feel a sense of relief and safeness. At some points, I was in denial that it happened. I could have taken such a fearful moment, mentally shut down and not ever fly again. At times, life throws us a curve ball. We can react to it with a meekness about us or pick up the bootstraps and carry on.

Trilogy Part 3

Relationships are defined as the way in which two or more concepts, objects, or people are connected, or the state of being connected. This could be someone you have an intimate relationship with, an acquaintance, or a friend. I believe they all are fostered over our lifetime. We are social animals; however, I don't believe we are savvy in our relationships. At least it takes time and work. There is no secret sauce. To me, any type of relationship requires self and situational assessment. My circle of friends may be bigger or smaller than someone else's.

One thing I really struggle with is my ability to understand how others intentionally hurt other individuals trying to fulfill their personal agenda. This is extremely hard for me. I know, I know, the battle is the Lord's. But I realize we have to create lanes of effort within ourselves to navigate these feelings.

As a single woman (divorced), I have wondered what my purpose is or why I was in a season with that individual. You see, life is a lesson. We grow from our experiences. We must take something from the relationships we are in to reach our purpose or even discover who we are as a woman. At times, we believe we are naive in relationships. Are we too trusting? Do we have expectations that are unrealistic? To want to be loved is not a bad thing. However, in relationships there is compromise, consideration, gratitude, adaptability, understanding and intentional works.

As woman, we think we are the fix-all in failures of any relationship. Removing that thinking from our minds is not easy. I found taking a step back to evaluate and then recognize required some soul-searching. We may have that ah-ha moment, but it may come years later when still trying to navigate relationships. I am truly a believer and optimist. I do spend a lot of my mental time trying to understand others. I would not say this is wasted time, but it is important to work on yourself. Don't occupy your brain space with unnecessary fuel. It is vital to our own health and comfort. God orders our steps in a way he knows we can handle them. He knows how much we can withstand. Colossians 3:23 Whatever you do, work at it with all your heart, as working for the Lord not for human masters.

We all have our shortcomings, and no one is perfect. Yes, we come with flaws. Having someone as a cheerleader in your life means so much. Someone willing to support you and have those difficult conversations in a loving way reaps healthy benefits. That also comes with loving unconditionally, whether you are giving or receiving for the right reasons. That is something I advocate for in a relationship. When you walk through life with someone who is as excited as you are, it helps keep the passion, and we become better versions of ourselves. How we react to outcomes of relationships is key to how we accept what God has planned for us.

If we stay in a sanitized space, how can we move forward and trust? If we remain guarded based on relationship experiences, how can we continue to bubble up within and take new relationships to new heights? We have the ability through self-confidence and realize that, as women, we are resilient. We can move through rejections in life and come out as the empowered, worthy women we can be. Don't get me wrong: it can be painstaking. We can be impatient. But remember, the timing is not ours.

At times, we have expectations of what a relationship should look like, feel like, flow like. It's okay, although disappointment comes when the relationship is at the macro-level and above. Let's be realistic. We don't have the bandwidth. It's a fast way to crash and burn in any relationship. As a woman who seeks success in her life, it includes all types of relationships. You must pray about it. You must let go and let God. You must recognize that God is enough and has framed you as a woman who he protects and welcomes with open arms. We just need to see it and receive it.

What comes with life lessons in relationships is that we change. We may not be that same person. Things come to light that we may not have dealt with before, or we put into place some savviness where we are no longer radio silent in our thinking or commitments to relationships. We have to pave the way, or there is no moving forward. We must live our life in a way full of the resources God has provided for us.

Let's not compare our relationships to others. Our relationship battles are different. Finding our way to build and to remove the grain-like obstacles can help us see things in a more positive light. Sometimes it may require a 360° assessment where we reach out to others and ask for advice on how they see us. It can be a hard pill to swallow, but the key to self-acceptance and willingness to be open minded. That sounds like relationships!

As creatures of habit, we tend to go searching or looking for relationships. It is in our nature to take care of others; hence, we have the need to be taken care of. There is absolutely nothing incorrect about that. Take into consideration the motive, what your intent may be, and remembering your why as a woman.

Over the years, I have shared my positive outlooks as well as those of others on life and self-attitude. Here are a few examples that help reframe our mind:

Challenges make you discover things about yourself that you never really knew. They're what make the instrument stretch – what make you go beyond the norm. - Cicely Tyson

Let joy be your continued feast. Make your life a prayer and in the midst of everything be always giving thanks. – Unknown

While it looks like things are out of control behind the scenes there is a God who hasn't surrendered his authority. – A.W. Tozer

WHO'S SLEEPING WITH YOUR HUSBAND TOO?

I would like to be known as an intelligent woman, a courageous woman, a loving women, a woman who teaches by being .– Maya Angelou

Keep the faith. Stay at the table if you're not standing on top of it. Take that balcony view!

Taking charge of your life means you can live your best life. Take it with active gratitude. It's that installment in life that will be well spent.

Chapter 11

Building Confidence Through Hair Therapy, Self-Care & Learning to Love Yourself

by Tiffany Posh

Your Hair Speaks Before You Do

The first thing I notice when someone walks into the room or when I meet them for the first time is their hair. It's not just because I'm a hair therapist; it's because hair can tell us a lot about a person. It can reflect their personality, their mood, and even their health.

As women, we tend to express ourselves through our hair, from trying different looks such as color, cuts, or trending styles. We also know that our hair can change depending on our mood. I'm sure you can think back over your life and can identify a certain hairstyle based on what was happening in your life at the time.

Well, just like our hair styles change with our moods, our hair itself changes. As a hair therapist for over 10 years, I've seen the toll that life cycles can take on our hair. From divorce to hormonal changes, sickness, kids leaving the house or moving back in, or taking care of loved ones at any moment, life can toss us an unexpected turn and we throw ourselves to the side.

Neglecting Yourself

Many women are guilty, including myself, of neglecting their hair in the face of life's challenges. We put our own needs and well-being on the back burner as we prioritize the needs of others. We don't realize what neglect can do to our hair. I'm sure you can think of times you looked in the mirror and realized you have neglected your hair – and yourself – for far too long.

Signs that your hair has been neglected come across in many ways. You may see your hair becoming thinner, shedding, damaged, crumble in your hand, dry to the touch, and now behaving the way it used to.

What are some of the things that come to mind when you notice you neglected your hair? Call a stylist? Grab a wig? Grab a hat? Run to the local beauty supply store to grab the newest product that claims to solve all your hair issues?

Well, I'm here to tell you that taking care of your hair can be a powerful form of self-care. It's something that you can control, even when life feels chaotic and overwhelming.

As women, we wear many hats, and it can be all too easy to neglect our own needs in the process. But by taking control of our hair, we're also taking control of our own lives, even when things around us are out of control.

But taking control of our hair isn't just about the physical act of caring for it. It's also about the mindset that we bring to it.

But when we take control of our hair, and we learn to love and care for our hair, we're also learning to love and care for ourselves. We're prioritizing our own needs and well-being, and in the process, we're empowering ourselves to be our best selves in all areas of our lives.

But, taking control of our hair isn't always easy. Life's challenges can take a toll on our hair, leaving it dry, brittle, or thinning.

As women, we often put the needs of others before our own, and as a result, we can suffer from low self-esteem and a lack of confidence. I know this all too well from my own journey.

Filling a Void

I remember my own hair journey and the validation I was seeking from men via my hair styles, from short cuts, to wearing hair extensions for longer or fuller hair or even a different texture. None of those things worked. I thought that I needed to impress a man for validation.

After years of failed dates and relationship attempts of looking for that "right one," I soon began to discover that I really didn't know what I was searching for. Being raised by a single mother, and with a father who was incarcerated for most of my life, I realized that I had no male figure to set the stage of how I should be treated or accepted by a man. If I had never seen a successful relationship or marriage, what was I basing my values on when searching?

As the years passed, the more I began to realize, through the stories of my clients, that all that glitters isn't gold. A lot of people who were together or married were unhappy. Here I was trying to find a husband, and many were trying to get rid of theirs. They were so unhappy but still felt obligated to stay, whether it was for the kids, finances, or simply the comfort of something familiar. I thought to myself that I would rather be single and happy than unhappily married. I still craved a partner but stopped actively searching for one.

I realized that I needed to focus on my own self-care and building my self-esteem from the inside out. Hair therapy played a big part in this process for me. By taking care of my hair, I was taking care of myself. Focusing on my hair, taking care of it, and expressing myself was a form of prioritizing self-care. It helped me to build my confidence and self-esteem.

When we focus on building our confidence and self-esteem from the inside out, we become more attractive to others in a different way. We are not seeking validation from a partner but rather radiating confidence and self-love. And when we love ourselves, we are more likely to attract healthy and fulfilling relationships, not just in marriage or with a life partner, but in all relationships with friends, colleagues, business partners, clubs, and all other social organizations.

Self-Care via Hair Therapy

Lately, we have heard the word self-care tossed around, but what does it really mean? After doing much soul searching and self-discovery, I would define self- care as anything you have control over that takes you away from everyday stresses, or things that will improve your mood or overall well-being. For some, it could be getting a massage, reading a book, exercising, eating healthy, or doing one of your favorite activities. For me, hair therapy has been a huge part of my self-care routine. It's a way to take some time for myself and focus on something that makes me feel good. And the best part is that when we prioritize self-care, we're better able to handle the stresses of daily life and have more energy to invest in our relationships.

Speaking of relationships, taking care of ourselves can actually improve them, too. When we put ourselves first, we're better equipped to show up for the people in our lives. We're more patient, empathetic, and understanding, which can lead to stronger and more positive relationships. Plus, when we take care of ourselves, we're setting an example for others and encouraging them to do the same.

When we don't prioritize self-care, we're more likely to feel stress, anxiety, and all kinds of other negative emotions. This can lead to a number of symptoms like headaches, muscle tension, and digestive issues, which will begin to manifest themselves in the hair and scalp.

One of the first things I discuss with a client who is experiencing hair loss or brittle thin hair is, "Is there any stress in your life?" and what may have changed drastically within the past year. Many don't realize that the major events happening in life play a very important role on your overall hair health. As the years go by and we experience different things - like empty nest syndrome, divorce, death, or changes in the environment, people coming in or out of the home, changes in careers, , or a change in your perception of self - all of these things will require you take a look at yourself and take a look at your hair.

The Power of Self-Care Through Hair Therapy

You may be thinking, "What is Hair Therapy?" Before I go on, let me explain exactly what hair therapy is. Hair therapy is when you consciously take steps to improve the overall health and appearance of your hair. This can be done by educating yourself on proper hair care, creating a new hair regimen, seeking out a hair therapist such as myself, and trying new styles that match your mood and your lifestyle. Hair therapy can help address issues such as hair loss, damage, and dandruff. Hair therapy can help keep your hair healthy and strong.

I use hair therapy with my clients during their session. After 10 years as a hair stylist, I began to recognize that something was missing. I wanted to offer something more than just a hairstyle, I wanted to offer a lifestyle to my clients. After hearing many stories and connecting with my clients on a personal level, I wanted to offer hope, confidence, and perseverance. If they couldn't have control over their life, they could have control over their hair. I called it hair therapy because the styling and conversation went beyond that day. Hair therapy takes commitment. It takes about 18-24 months to get your hair to its healthiest potential.

Taking care of your hair can have a huge impact on our confidence. When your hair looks good, we feel good, and that can spill over into other areas of your life. But hair therapy is about more than just the physical appearance of our hair. It's about the emotional and mental benefits that come with taking care of ourselves.

Hair therapy can be a form of self-care that helps us build confidence and self-esteem. When we take the time to care for our hair, we're sending a message to ourselves that we're worth the effort. We're saying, "I value myself and I deserve to look and feel good." And when we feel good about ourselves, we're more likely to take on new challenges and pursue our goals.

It's not just about the external benefits, either. Hair therapy can also have a positive impact on our mental health. When we're stressed, anxious, or dealing with negative emotions, taking some time to care for ourselves can be a great way to relax and recharge. It's a chance to focus on something positive and take a break from the things that are weighing us down.

Of course, it's not just about having a good hair day. Building confidence and self-esteem takes time and effort. But hair therapy can be a powerful tool in our self-care routine that helps us on that journey. And when we're feeling good about ourselves, the possibilities are endless. We can pursue our dreams, take on new challenges, and build the kind of life we want to live.

Taking control of our hair is not always easy, though. Life's challenges can take a toll on our hair, leaving it dry, brittle, or thinning. Hormonal changes during pregnancy or menopause can cause changes in hair texture and thickness. And let's not forget the effect that stress can have on our hair; it can cause hair loss or make it more prone to breakage.

But just as life's challenges can impact our hair, our hair can also impact how we navigate those challenges. When our hair looks and feels good, we feel more confident and empowered to tackle whatever comes our way. And when we prioritize self-care through our hair care routine, we're also setting the stage for self-care in all other areas of our lives.

As a hair therapist, I've worked with countless women over the years to help them revitalize and care for their hair, no matter what life has thrown their way. I've helped women with hair loss caused by chemotherapy or hormonal changes, as well as women who simply want to revitalize their hair after years of neglect.

When we feel good about ourselves, we radiate positive energy. By regularly taking care of our hair, we can build confidence and self-esteem, which can attract positive people and experiences into our lives. Hair therapy can also provide a way to express our individuality and creativity, which can further enhance our self-confidence.

By taking care of ourselves through hair therapy, we are better able to face life's challenges with a positive attitude and mindset.

Tips for Practicing Self-Care Through Hair Therapy
Are you ready to take control of your hair? Do you want heads to turn in a positive way because you radiate confidence? Whether you are wearing your hair long, short, curly, straight, blonde, black or any color and style in between, wear it with a sense of self-worth.

Here are a few tips and takeaways that will help you on your hair journey.

Schedule regular appointments with a hair therapist/or stylist. Make sure you find someone who fits your lifestyle and personality and who takes the time out to learn you as a person. This will also help you to establish a long-term relationship with a stylist who values you.

You may need to find a few stylists. If you like to try different looks like myself, have your list ready; not all stylists are experts in all styling. For example, someone who is amazing at hair care may not be the same person who is good at braids, color, or extensions.

Your number 1 priority above any styling is to keep your own hair healthy and looking its best.

Experiment with different hairstyles and colors to express your individuality and creativity.

Use hair care products that are formulated with essential vitamins and nutrients to nourish your hair and scalp.

In addition to hair therapy, I am also the founder of my own hair care line "Posh Hair Therapy" which provides the essential building blocks to strengthen, repair & grow healthy hair, allowing clients to take control of their own hair therapy journey right at home.

Remember to Take time for yourself to relax and unwind, and to focus on your own well-being.

Conclusion

In conclusion, as a hair therapist and someone who has been on a personal journey of self-discovery, I've learned that the power of self-love and self-care cannot be overstated. Too often, women wear many hats, including that of wife, mother, and worker, and in the process, neglect their own needs and well-being.

But as I've learned through my own experiences and those of my clients, self-care and self-love are not optional. They are essential for living a fulfilling and happy life.

Through our hair, we can learn a lot about ourselves and our relationship with ourselves. If we're constantly criticizing and hating our hair, it may be a sign that we're not valuing ourselves as we should. But when we learn to love and care for our hair, we're also learning to love and care for ourselves.

As a hair therapist, I'm grateful for the opportunity to help my clients cultivate self-love and self-acceptance. By valuing themselves and their hair, they're able to cultivate a deeper sense of self-worth and confidence. That is truly powerful.

In the end, the most important relationship we have is the one we have with ourselves. By valuing ourselves and our worth, we're able to attract positivity and happiness into our lives, and that is the greatest validation of all.

Hair therapy is a powerful tool for practicing self-care and building confidence. By taking care of our hair, we can improve our overall well-being and radiate positive energy. I encourage you to prioritize self-care through hair therapy, and to make it a regular part of your self-care routine.

I'm passionate about helping women take control of their hair and, in the process, take control of their own lives. By prioritizing self-care and self-love, we can empower ourselves to be our best selves, no matter what life throws our way.

Chapter 12

Understanding Who You Are

by Dr. Paula B. Miller

It's safe to say you have a lot on your plate. Between work, family, friends, and other responsibilities that always seem to need your immediate attention, it can be difficult to give yourself the time and space you deserve. You've been told by others that in order to be successful in life or at work, you must know who you are and what is important to you. But how exactly do we go about doing this?

In this chapter, I will show you the basic steps for developing a prosperous soul: understanding that we are what we want out of life and finding ways of integrating those desires with our current reality. When we are in touch with whom we are, our inner guidance system works much more effectively and consistently.

Before getting started with the steps of developing a prosperous soul, it's important to understand that this process is not something you complete and then leave behind. Instead, it is a life-long journey of exploration and discovery. The steps below will give you some direction and tools for getting started, but you may find that along the way, your priorities change or new interests emerge. With experience, patience, reflection, and self-awareness, you will be able to deepen your understanding of yourself as you continue learning about life's many mysteries.

Step 1: Become Aware of Your Self-Talk

The first step in the process of developing a prosperous soul is to become aware of your internal self-talk. We are largely unaware of the thoughts that go through our minds and lead us to feelings and actions. As a result, much of what we do is based on habits that were formed unconsciously.

We think we are making conscious decisions, but if you dig deeper, you will find that many of your thoughts, feelings, and actions are not in line with who you are and what's important to you.

There are many ways to explore the inner workings of your mind and find out what is going on when you make a conscious decision or start thinking about something. For instance, you can pay attention to your physical and emotional responses to different people, places, or events. You can make small changes in your daily routine and observe how this makes you feel. You can write in a journal about a particular topic, feeling, or experience and then reflect on what you wrote later. You can also practice mindfulness methods such as meditation to gain deeper insight into the workings of your mind.

Step 2: Identify What's Important to You

Building on your awareness of internal self-talk, the next step is to become aware of what's important to you in life. This will help you identify what you value most and, in turn, help create clarity about your goals and priorities. I've found that there are three effective ways of doing this.

The first method is to identify your beliefs. What do you believe to be true about yourself, the world, and the people around you? During your practice of meditation or mindfulness, pay attention to what thoughts or images come up for you. You can also write about them in a journal or brainstorm in small groups. Sometimes, our unconscious beliefs may be working against us even though we don't realize it. For instance, I once had a client who was very smart, intelligent, and talented, but she convinced herself (and others) that she was not good at anything, despite her achievements. This belief was so deeply ingrained that it created a huge obstacle in her personal and professional life.

The second method is to reflect on your life story. If you had to describe your life in one sentence, what would it be? What's the main theme or message that runs through it? Is there any insight hidden in there that you can discover by taking some time to reflect?

The third method is to identify your values and goals. What are the things that you value most in life? What do you want to achieve in your personal and/or professional life? Where do you see yourself five years from now? What relationships or experiences do you want to have, and what kind of person do you want to be?

Step 3: Commit to Who You Are and What's Important to You

The purpose of the third step is to bring your insights and goals into your conscious awareness. This will help create alignment between who you are, what's important to you, and how your thoughts, feelings, and actions line up with those ideals. It will also serve as a motivator for bringing them into reality.

To start, make a list (on paper or in your mind) of the things that are important to you. These may include areas related to your personal life, such as relationships, health, and spirituality. It may also include areas related to your professional life like your career, financials, and the way you spend your free time. For example, it is common for people to say that they want to travel more but then neglect this desire by not saving money for it or putting it off until some distant date in the future. Instead, I encourage people to start by taking small actions in this area of their lives as soon as possible. This might include making a decision to give a portion of your income to charity or setting aside a certain amount of time each week for exercise.

Once you've identified the things that are important to you, make a commitment to bring them into life. For instance, if it is something related to your personal life, such as relationships, commit yourself to make decisions that will bring these areas into alignment with who you are and what's important. This might include devoting some of your free time each week to connecting with people in meaningful ways that are aligned with who you are and what's important in life.

Do the same with things that are important to you in your professional life. What kinds of decisions will it take to make these areas of your life align with who you are and what's important? How can you change your work habits, communication, or relationships in order to bring them into alignment?

Step 4: Take the Small Steps to Bring It into Reality

The final step is taking action on your commitment by taking small moves that will bring the areas of your life into alignment with who you are and what's important. This might include taking those actions that were discussed in the previous step, such as saving money for a trip, making time for exercise, or devoting free time each week to connecting with people. By doing so, you will make it more likely for your vision of who you want to be to become a reality.

By being true to who you are and what's important to you, you will act on your values and goals with less resistance. You will find yourself becoming the person that you want to be and living the life that you want to live. This is a very fulfilling way of living because it helps you bring more of your true self into the world.

You are your own special creation, formed in the image and likeness of one of the most powerful beings in the entire universe. Recognizing this truth can help you on your journey through life. You are not a mistake or an accident, and you were never "unwanted" or overlooked by God. You were created by Him with a specific purpose and destiny in mind for you—to be blessed, prosperous, and joyfully happy!

So start today to discover just how richly blessed your life is going to be!

Most people don't even know what their goals are for this lifetime. They hope to get rich or famous but don't have any idea how they might do that. They don't know what their purpose in life is. What is it? How will you fulfill it? Don't you deserve to know this information?

Your true identity as a being of light was revealed to me by a great and mighty Light Being named Master Orion, who came to me in my dreams one night and told me that my soul's purpose is to help others discover their true divinity. Your divine soul essence contains the purest form of love imaginable because it was programmed with perfect love for everyone on earth—including yourself! You were created with a divine purpose, which means that you have many unique and special gifts and talents that only you can bring to bear on your journey through life.

The light within you is the purest form of love because you were created with a divine purpose.

You possess what I call the "Golden Thread" of Self, which is a golden cord that runs through all of your cells and connects your consciousness with every cell in your body. This Golden Thread is like a computer network that keeps your mind/soul essence connected to its divine source, just as computers are technologically connected to the Internet (the universal brain) through wires and other devices. In other words, you are the connection point between this dimension and many different dimensions.

This is why you have access to infinite wisdom and endless knowledge within your mind/soul. In the 144,000-year cycle of the earth's ascension into the 7th-dimensional reality of Christ's consciousness, you will be empowered to expand your consciousness and use your mind/soul as a portal to expand your awareness into other dimensions, learning even more about God.

All of this information is right there inside that "Golden Thread" of light that runs throughout all of your cells. You can access your divinity and completely shift your consciousness into your true reality at any time. It is essential that you exercise this power of creation daily to stay in alignment with your soul's oneness with God so that you will achieve the best results for yourself.

The Golden Thread of Self that connects you to your divine source contains your soul's purpose for this life.

UNDERSTANDING WHO YOU ARE

It is a simple formula that helps people overcome the fear and confusion they experience when considering their infinite potential, power, gifts, talents, and abilities, as well as their divine destiny:

1) Acknowledge Your Divine Soul Purpose by writing down these four words: Infinite Potential; Power; Gifts; Talents; Abilities.
2) Affirm your eternal divinity and do the following daily: Ask yourself, "What part of me or my life can I use to bring more light?" If you find no answer, consider what you can take to use in service. You might just find that you have something to add to someone else's life to make them happy and uplifted.
3) Create a new goal: Step one is done! Now write down this new goal by taking one step forward and writing it down.
4) Write down how you are going to accomplish this new goal every day.

By following these four steps, you will begin to develop the prosperity consciousness that is your divine birthright and is necessary to bring more light into your life. This is how you will tune in and transform yourself so that you can attract what you want. This is how you will learn to use the Golden Thread of Self within your body/brain as an infinite power source for manifesting all of your dreams.

You have everything you need within your own light, but it takes a certain amount of courage, which I call "Soul-Courage," if you are going to manifest all that God wants for your life.

Biographies
Meet the Authors

Dr. Jeri Godhigh

Dr. Jeri Godhigh is a prominent public speaker, driven leader, real estate maven, best-selling author, and life-enhancing consultant in the Acworth, Georgia community. She captivates audiences with her undeniable charisma, engaging demeanor, powerful dictation and genuine passion for enhancing the legacy of generational wealth. Dr. Godhigh is a certified Trauma and Life Coach, is Founder and CEO of The Godhigh Agency, of Godhigh & Associates Realty Company, and of Josie's Girls Lead, a nonprofit organization geared toward the betterment and building of women in various walks of life. She turned a love for the art of real estate into a career that has continued to flourish for over 17 years. Recently, Dr. Godhigh was awarded the

Presidential Lifetime Achievement Award for her humanitarian efforts and commitment to helping Georgia families.

Hailing from Washington, DC, Jeri always had a desire to be an avid educator. She attended real estate school after falling in love with the art of selling real estate. She became a licensed realtor and saw several opportunities in the South. As a result, she moved to Acworth, Georgia to enhance her real estate brand. The move offered Jeri an opportunity to dive into the expansive Georgia real estate market, which at that time, had little representation from African American women. Jeri truly enjoys helping millennials navigate the home buying experience and uses her knowledge and relatability to engage with them. So much so, she is not only an active real estate broker, but also a certified instructor with American Real Estate University where she teaches the fundamentals of sales.

Godhigh has been recognized for her work in Formidable Magazine as a 'Queen of Real Estate', and has graced the cover of many well known magazines. Her servitude toward her community includes operating as an Ordained Minister and volunteer work within the counties and State of Georgia as well as serving on many organizations as Board of Director. In her downtime, Godhigh loves spending quality time with her family and close friends. Dr. Godhigh will be releasing her third book with the newest book entitled 'Who's Sleeping with Your Husband Too? A Woman's Guide to Live Life Her Way' which is a collaborative book co-authored with powerful leading women destined to be another Best-Selling Book. You can find her latest published work in bookstores and major retailers. Additionally, Dr. Godhigh's new TV Show 'Live on Purpose Talk Show by Dr. Jeri & Chaun' will be airing in March 2023.

Dr. Jeri, along with her daughter Jamia Ponder, curated Jeri & Jamia: Unfiltered, a powerful movement and coaching program created to help mother-daughter relationships to heal and break generational curses. They also launched the Unfiltered podcast as an additional resource in offering healing and advice. Dr. Godhigh continues to shatter glass ceilings with her generational legacy intentions, and continues to make both her family, and herself, proud.

Jamia Ponder

Jamia Ponder is the founder and creator of "The Mrs. Beside ™," a movement and safe space dedicated to celebrating women, wives, and mothers standing beside and never behind their spouse. The movement celebrates women and encourages them to walk in their full purpose which starts by putting them first. From working full-time jobs, kid pick up, drop off, grocery shopping, planning, bills, budgeting, chauffeuring and an expected chandelier swing from time to time, Ponder knows the toll it can take and what it takes to wear the many hats of the home.

Ponder is an active mother of three and the wife of a medical physician, and she has been there every step of the way! Ponder spent years supporting her husband through medical school and working numerous jobs just to put food on the table. Taking on the primary role of budgeting, child rearing, and making preparations for the unseen and unknown inadvertently left her in a secondary role in her own life. Determined not to see other women leave themselves in the background of their own lives, Ponder set out on a personal journey to heal and, in turn, empower women to reclaim their purpose and reignite their passion.

In addition to her work on the "The Mrs. Beside ™" movement, Ponder is a Certified Life & Wife Coach dedicated to helping women and wives activate their strength, acknowledge their areas of fulfillment and walk into their purpose as individuals. Ponder is an author in the powerful anthology, Deeper Women Teach, released in May of 2021. She partnered with her mother, Jeri Godhigh, unveiling Jeri and Jamia: Unfiltered, a powerful and necessary platform, created to help mothers & daughters heal and break generational curses.

Jamia Ponder is available for interviews, appearances, and speaking engagements. All media and booking inquiries should be directed to themrsbesidethemd@gmail.com.

Stephany Tullis

Stephany Tullis is a *USA Today* and Amazon Bestselling Author of women's and inspirational fiction. She is also a small business management consultant, educator, publisher, freelance writer, and contributor to several peer reviewed journal articles. She has written 21 books and short stories, including her contribution to the Soul Deep Anthology, *My Soul Speaks, Who am I?*; the award winning first novel, *The Master's Plan*; and the Angelica Mason Series that includes *Blue Lady's MISSION Under FIRE*, a fast-paced biographical political allegory centered around true events in Upstate New York.

She has a graduate degree in Public Service Administration from Russell Sage College and 27 years' experience with the New York State government where she started as a New York State Management Intern.

She is the recipient of the following awards: Governor's Tribute to African American Leaders of Excellence, NYS Commissioner of Civil Service Merit Award, Creative Excellence in Benefits Award (Nominee), and Who's Who in the Kennesaw Business Association.

A New York native, she currently lives in Georgia, where she never misses an opportunity to travel with family and friends.

You can reach me on my social media platforms:
Email: stephanytwrites@gmail.com
Website: https://www.stephany-tullis.com/
Twitter: https://twitter.com/StephanyTullis
Facebook: https://www.facebook.com/StephanyTullis2
BookBub: https://www.bookbub.com/authors/stephany-tullis

Miracle C. Austin

Miracle Austin is a highly accomplished professional with a wealth of experience in both the corporate world and the field of love and relationship coaching. She holds a bachelor's degree from SNHU and is set to complete her MBA from the University of Alabama at Birmingham.

Miracle has been happily married for 32 years and counting, having been with her partner for 38 years. She is the proud mother of two adult sons and a grandmother to three beautiful grandchildren.

With over 30 years of experience in the corporate sector, Miracle's true passion lies in helping others achieve success in their relationships. As a love relationship coach, she has been working with women in marriages for over 5 years, helping them to navigate the complexities of building and maintaining healthy, fulfilling partnerships.

Miracle is a published author, having co-authored Who's Sleeping with Your Husband Too? and is set to release an upcoming book in July. She has also been a featured speaker at several events and has appeared on various podcasts.

Through her coaching practice, Miracle is committed to empowering women by providing them with personalized support, resources, and a community to help them thrive both as individuals and partners. She believes that every woman deserves to experience the joy and fulfillment of everlasting love, and she is dedicated to helping them achieve this goal.

Lisa R. Robinson Patterson

Lisa R. Robinson Patterson has been married for forty years to her husband, Raynard. Lisa has six adult children: Candice, Lawrence, Lamar, Larnelle, twins (LaNard and Cara). Raynard and Lisa have six grandchildren.

Lisa is a retired employee of Jefferson County Schools in Charles Town, WV. Upon graduation from high school, she worked in the following positions: federal and state government as secretary, secretary in the loan department at the Continental Federal Bank, at home mother for 10 years, a volunteer with the Jefferson County School System as a mentor to third grade students, substitute teacher's aide, and full-time school bus driver for 15 years until retirement in June 2022.

Lisa's hobbies and interests include caregiving for family members and those in need, sewing, crafts, painting, interior decorating, canning, gardening, and jewelry making. She has earned certificates in CPR and First Aid. Lisa also has a Class B CDL License and continues to drive upon request.

Lisa's purpose and aspiration is to focus on herself and what God has planned for her at this time in her life.

"For we are His workmanship, created in Christ Jesus unto good works, which God hath before ordained that we should walk in them." Ephesians 2:10 KJV

Jolie Rashawn

Jolie Rashawn is originally from South Florida; she currently resides in the Dallas/Fort Worth area.

She is the badd azz, fine, fierce, and focused trailblazer who not only talks the talk, but she definitely walks the walk!

Feature in 2022/2023 Her Fire Magazine
The G Magazine feature 2022/2023
Feature in Santana Global 2022
Awarded the 2022 Woman of Truth Award
Podcast Truth-Full Conversation with Jolie Rashawn

She is an enthusiastic business owner, wife, and woman of faith who loves God, an ordained Minister, Certified Motivational Speaker, Certified Life Coach, Publish Modeled, 5x Bestselling Author, among other things.
Her core essentials are faith, love, and family. Her foundation is centered around two scriptures: Proverbs 3:5-6; Trust in the Lord with all thine heart and lean not unto your own understanding. In all thy ways acknowledge Him and He shall direct thy path; and Jeremiah 29:11; I know the plans I have for you, declares the Lord, plans to prosper you and not harm you, plans to give you hope and a future.

She is known as the CFB (The Chief Focused Boss) She is a passionate vessel looking for 1 million women that she can pour into. Her mission is to help women get serious and more focused about their worth, while becoming in harmony with themselves, helping them to strategize, get healed, be impactful and transform - in other words, she helps women get S.H.I.T done!

She is a ticking time bomb full of love, compassion, words of healing, and teaching. She is transparent, always putting God first and making sure she walks in His favor and in His will. She is one of those people you need on your team, your personal hype woman to cheer you on to the finish line. Through her struggles, she has learned some key elements that she uses to coach and uplift women into a greater awareness of focus and purpose! She is here to guide that woman into her Boss Up Season!, taking charge of her life and walking in what's been inside of her from the beginning.

Deena C. M. Wingard

Deena C. M. Wingard is a teacher, preacher, pastor, writer, and attorney. Her mission is to spread the good news that Jesus loves us just as we are. Yet, God loves us too much to have us stay in our brokenness, so Pastor Deena strives to tell a dying world about God's transformative power. She and her husband, Pastor Elgin L. Wingard, Sr., are excited about all God has in store for them as they walk together in their calling.

Pastor Deena Wingard was called by God to "Go" and spread the gospel in year 2000. It took her ten years to fully walk into that calling when she received the mantle of Minister in 2010. Due to her faithfulness and service, Bishop Gary Hawkins, Sr. ordained her as Elder in 2012. She has served in various churches over the years and in many capacities, including Sunday School Teacher, Church Planter, Corporate Prayer Leader, Christian Education Head, Associate Pastor, and Founder and CEO of Your Reasonable Service Ministries, LLC.

While Pastor Deena is grateful that God saw fit for her to obtain her Juris Doctorate Degree and a Master of Divinity, she wisely recognizes that what truly equips her to do the work of Christ is the Holy Spirit who rules, rests, and abides within her. As she accepts the calling of Pastor on her life, she still marvels at how God can turn dry and seemingly dead lives into vessels full of The Living Water and overflowing with abundance. She brings this same humble passion to the church she birthed: Shekinah Greater Love Tabernacle, Inc. (SGLT). SGLT serves to equip God's people to do God's work and build up the body of Christ, per Ephesians 4:12.

Pastor Deena published her first book, Almost, in August 2022. Additionally, God has placed many other books in her spirit to write; thus, she is excited about bringing to life everything God directs.

For speaking engagements and to connect with Pastor Deena:

Facebook: @Ministering2MinistersForum
Twitter: @DeenaCMWingard
Instagram: @pastor_dwingard
Websites: YourReasonableService.com; ShekinahGreaterlove.com

Alexandra Sanders

Alexandra Sanders is a Commercial Banking Strategist, Sales Professional, Women in Leadership Lead, keynote speaker, and serial learner.

She has demonstrated a history of success working in strong sales environments within consumer and business banking while maintaining a lead position in women in leadership and colleague mentorship.

Alexandra is a graduate of Purdue University Magna Cumme Laude, where she majored in Business. She currently lives in Jacksonville with her partner.

Chaun Pinkston

Chaun Pinkston, entrepreneur, film director, and ordained minister, is a native of Southwest Atlanta. She has a passion for people and the arts and began her pursuit of higher living at a very young age.

Chaun is President and CEO of Seedtime Productions, Inc., a media arts entertainment company specializing in film and video production. She and her husband, Roderick, co-own Pinkston Automotive Services Group and North Henry Auto Body, both located in Stockbridge, Georgia.

Chaun is the founder and chair of the Atlanta chapter of the Alliance of Women Directors, an organization helping women advance behind the camera in film and television.

As a minister, Chaun utilizes her more than 25 years of experience in marriage, business, and ministry to encourage others to pursue higher living in God. Chaun is a passionate and practical speaker with a natural ability to inspire others. She shares transparently in the areas of marriage, family, business, and leadership.

One of her greatest delights is sharing in ministry service with her husband and their three children, Choan, Camille, and Camrine.

Chaun graduated from Georgia State University, earning a BA in Film and Media. She is currently pursuing a Master of Divinity from Emory University's school of theology, Candler.

Joe Hunter

Jae Hunter is a mom of nine. With a blended family, she has learned a thing or two about major social issues, which she constantly shares about on her social pages. Jae graduated from Ashford University with a degree in psychology and a minor in English. Two of her passions have always been people and the written word.

Jae is an internationally published hair and makeup artist, and when she's not working on her business, she runs a Neurology clinic as well as a logistics company that she co-owns with her husband. She focuses on helping women find their purpose and gives of her talent when she can by donating her time and skills to local charity events.

Jae is currently participating in Embrace Grace, a non-profit ministry that assists young soon-to-be moms. She is also partaking in The Great Gala – a yearly fashion show that donates all their proceeds to The Stepping Stones Foundation, an emergency housing facility that assists young displaced people.

Jae started writing poetry at a very young age and received her first publication at the tender age of 15. She has never lost the gift of the written word and is currently working on her first book, so stay tuned for that one to drop soon.

Dr. Donna Newman

Dr. Donna Newman is passionate about education and creating a learning environment of self-awareness and strong confidence. She holds a Doctor of Executive Leadership from the University of Charleston, WV School of Business and Leadership. She has spent much of her life mentoring others on a professional and personal level. She believes we are led by the conversations and networking opportunities in front of us. Through this writing, she hopes to inspire other like-minded women to pursue a life guided by true motivation, persistence, leadership, and love, while remembering to keep God in the details of it all. She was recognized for her accomplishment in paving the way and creating history as the first black title holder on a local and national stage. She aspires to continue to serve in a consultative platform and take her leadership skills to a university setting. Living in the Eastern Panhandle of West Virginia, Donna loves to serve the Lord and enjoys traveling and spending time with her family.

Tiffany Posh

Tiffany Posh, also known as DMVHAIRDOCTOR, is a highly respected hair therapist, entrepreneur, community volunteer, speaker, and author. She has over 10 years of experience in the hair care industry and grew up in New Jersey.

Tiffany's career began as a hairstylist in New Jersey, where she quickly discovered her passion for hair care. Over the years, she has honed her skills and expanded her knowledge to become a hair therapist, specializing in hair therapy and restoration. She has owned and operated several salons. Her expertise and dedication to her craft have earned her recognition as a leading expert in the industry.

In addition to her work as a hair therapist, Tiffany is also a successful entrepreneur, owning and operating her own hair care product line. Her products are innovative, ground-breaking, and designed to promote healthy hair growth, transformation, and maintenance. Her business has been recognized for its excellence and has been featured in several publications, including Asbury Park Press.

As a sought-after speaker and guest lecturer, Tiffany has shared her expertise and insights with audiences at universities and events around the world. She inspires and motivates people to pursue their passions and interests and has become a leading voice in the hair care and personal empowerment industries.

As an author, Tiffany focuses on hair care and personal empowerment. Her writing is engaging, informative, and inspiring, reflecting her commitment to helping people feel confident and beautiful through their hair.

Despite her busy schedule, Tiffany remains committed to giving back to her community. She volunteers her time and resources to support local organizations and initiatives focused on empowering young people and women.

Tiffany's diverse range of accomplishments and her unwavering dedication to her craft and community have earned her a loyal following and numerous accolades. Her book tour provides an opportunity for her to share her knowledge, expertise, and experiences with others who are passionate about hair care and personal empowerment. Whether you are a hairstylist, a hair enthusiast, or someone looking to learn more about natural hair care, Tiffany's book and tour will leave you inspired and informed.

Dr. Paula B. Miller

Dr. Paula B. Miller is the CEO of I AM Dr. Paula B. Miller, a platform that draws from a well of years of experience in being successful and a master of life.

As a high achiever herself, she believes strongly in people understanding their self-worth and value while teaching them how to develop a prosperous soul and life. She is also an expert at teaching ways to avoid unhealthy coping mechanisms, minimize stress and prevent other health problems. All of these have made her seek out individuals looking to be a better version of themselves and relieve themselves of their past pain. Her goal is to help people grow and unlock their full potential so they can realize all the things they are capable of that they did not know.

Special Note

Speak Your Peace

Have you ever been in a stormy situation in which it seemed as if the devil was attempting to stir up everything in your life such as contention, hurt and wounds, anger, fear and the works? It is during these turbulent times that you see you exactly for who you are. How you respond and act in those very moments reveals to you, Who You Are. And so, the question remains, who is your husband sleeping with? Are you bitter? Are you hurting from past or present hurts in a negative way? Or are you thriving and redeemed? It is very clear where you are in your emotional state when trying times come knocking at your door.

It is imperative for us to constantly check and recheck ourselves. You, me - we cannot do it alone. It only comes when we are truly honest with ourselves and begin to do the deep work within us to become fully healed. Once we are healed, we can develop and foster healthy relationships. It is only then that we will see open doors and opportunities that will propel us to the next level in life walking a freer life.

God has made me and blessed me! He has clothed me with His glory and has presented me as good. I am the gift! I am a woman of wisdom. I know what to do at the time I need to do it. I have God-given insight. I protect my family from the enemy, and I intercede on their behalf. I am rooted and grounded in love and because of that my faith is strong and it does not waiver.

I am fulfilling my purpose in God and fruit abounds in every area of my life. I willingly and lovingly submit my will to God. I trust in God confidently to take care of me. God is my protector and my refuge. God has empowered me to fulfill my purpose. He has established me in His Word and His promises are manifested daily in my life, and I receive all that I am entitled to under my covenant with God.

I am free from fear, doubt, and worry. I renew my mind with the Word of God and my spirit is rejuvenated through my daily fellowship with Jesus. I am a woman of power, great presence, high position and prosperity.

I look well to the ways of my home. The Lord will exalt me in due season, and my hands will always reap the fruit of increase. In Jesus Name…Amen!

Works Cited:
https://www.psychologytoday.com/us/blog/love-and-sex-in-the-digital-age/201912/how-adverse-childhood-experiences-affect-you-adult.

Moore, Ayra. "Single-Parent Family Social Problems." Hello Motherhood, 28 November 2018, https://www.hellomotherhood.com/single-parent-family-social-problems-8266822.html. Accessed 15 March 2023.

Wigington, Patti. "The Cult of Domesticity: Definition and History." ThoughtCo, 16 October 2021, https://www.thoughtco.com/cult-of-domesticity-4694493. Accessed 10 March 2023.

"Women in the 1950s (article) | 1950s America." Khan Academy, https://www.khanacademy.org/humanities/us-history/postwarera/1950s-america/a/women-in-the-1950s. Accessed 10 March 2023.

Zane, Matthew. "What Percentage of The Workforce Is Female? [2023] – Zippia." Zippia, 1 March 2022, https://www.zippia.com/advice/what-percentage-of-the-workforce-is-female/. Accessed 10 March 2023.

Made in the USA
Columbia, SC
15 July 2024

38419877R00093